The Making of a Man:
True Manhood Lies in the Process

AKAI JACKSON AND ALLAN SOBIE

Copyright © 2016 Akai Jackson and Allan Sobie

All rights reserved. No part of this publication may be reproduced or transmitted in any form or by any electronic or mechanical means including photo copying, recording, or any information storage and retrieval system now known or to be invented, without permission in writing from the publisher or the author.

All Scripture quotations are from The ESV Bible (The Holy Bible, English Standard Version) copyright © 2001 by Crossway Bibles, a publishing ministry of Good News Publishers. The ESV text has been reproduced in cooperation with and by permission of Good News Publishers. Unauthorized reproduction of this publication is prohibited. All rights reserved.

ISBN: 978-1-945975-02-8

Published by EA Books Publishing a division of
Living Parables of Central Florida, Inc. a 501c3
EABooksPublishing.com

Some of the thoughts, ideas, and definitions for this book are based on original Men's Fraternity material of Dr. Robert Lewis, as well as contributing writers of 33 Series Volume 1; A Man and his Design & 33 Series Volume 2 A Man and his Story: John Bryson, Brian Carter, and Tierce Green.

DEDICATION

We would like to thank all of our loved ones for their continued support throughout this process and for all their encouragement along the way. For it is them who sharpen us the most and make us strive to continue to grow into the men God created us to be. To our families for setting the foundation of faith and for their constant encouragement throughout our manhood process. To all the coaches and mentors that pushed us, and helped develop us along our journey. To all the men, our brothers, that have lent us their ears for suggestions, their hearts for truth, and their hands to pull us into manhood.

CONTENTS

	Introduction: The Importance of Brotherhood & Unity	1
I	What Am I Doing Here?	5
II	Built by Design	9
III	How You Arrived	15
IV	Defining Moments	19
V	Your Gut Telling You Something	29
VI	Mindset, Heart Set, Health Set	33
VII	From Good to Great and Beyond	37
VIII	The Architecture of Your Body	45
IX	What Do You See When You Look in the Mirror	49
X	Heart Determines Life	61
XI	In Sync in There	73
XII	The Language Your Body Speaks	75
XIII	Your Influence Means Everything	99
XIV	What Lies Beneath	105
	Notes	119
	About the Authors	121

INTRODUCTION: THE IMPORTANCE OF BROTHERHOOD & UNITY

Climbing a mountain or sailing the wildest seas alone is a difficult - even dangerous - idea. Attempting to get through life alone is also not recommended. In the same way an actual mountain climber would need to be connected with another person for safety and support, or just as the captain needs another set of eyes and ears as he embarks to the world unknown; we need a community around us. We need people to help us stay the course, and hold us accountable. Having a partner or a community intrinsically attached to us is priceless when we fail, fall, slip, struggle, falter, or stray on our journey towards our ultimate goals.

One of the biggest mistakes we believe you could make is not share valuable information with a partner or community - to attempt to do life in isolation. Isolation leads to confusion. Confusion brings about chaos. The goal of this book is to help you connect the dots to your life. We hope and pray you connect your mind to your heart and your heart to your body over the next 30-60 days. By doing so, you will have completely transformed. You will have the platform laid out for your success as a son, father, husband, brother, and most importantly as a man.

We want to encourage you- Almost half of the children born today will grow up in a household without a (their) father. We have found that every man needs other men rooting for them and cheering for them. Every man needs a pat on the back every once in awhile, on his quest to find himself.

We want to give insight- The two ways you learn are from 1) pain and 2) insight. Reading this book, know that we have walked in your shoes and learned from our pain. Having a partner or a community of men around you helps you gain perspective. Other men can assist you. They can help you discover areas in your life blind to you, in order to help you avoid extreme mistakes.

We want to make your journey towards the ultimate vast- Sharing life with a partner or community will allow you to capture amazing moments and gain support when you struggle.

We want to critique and give you feedback- We all need people around us who will lean in and be completely truthful with us as we grow. Remember this; you are the average of the sum of the five people you spend the most time with. We know and understand no one can convince you to peel back some of those painful layers. No one can force you to face some of the pain/baggage you have been carrying throughout your lifetime. However, throughout this journey, you will find that you feel less suppressed. You will be able to think more clearly. Although it will be remonstrant and terrifying, it will be well worth it and priceless.[1]

THE MAKING OF A MAN: TRUE MANHOOD LIES IN THE PROCESS

I. WHAT AM I DOING HERE?

MIND-*"The heart of man plans his way, but The Lord establishes his steps."*
Proverbs 16:9 ESV

Do you find yourself living a "less than life"? Are the walls in your life slowly inching in closer to you each day? When you look at your life, do you only see chaos? Are you struggling to find meaning or the purpose you were created for? If you can identify with any of these questions, you are not alone. Countless men live a friendless life. They are disconnected and lonely. Sadly, this is the reality we face, today. Our world is in desperate need and desire for better men to show up. How can you get there, if you lack clarity or vision? In order for you to find out where you are going, you must first identify and understand where you currently are. Most men are in a state of complete disbelief, which leads to confusion. Men default to childish boyhood tendencies, and often times question when does manhood even begin. Not knowing when manhood actually begins causes men to resort to guessing.[2] They are generally quite disappointed with their lives. They have a deep burning desire for more. The weight of responsibility and the burden of a family; life becomes more about duty and work than actually LIVING. Men are lonely with a decrease of deep intimacy in many areas of their lives. They have no deep intrinsic connections despite knowing everyone, because no one really – fully - knows them. Men have unresolved pain. They are bruised, battered, and beaten from head to toe. Most do not even know why. The state of manhood today is drifting as men are just roughly going through the motions. Do you react to life instead of purposefully making decisions for life? You need to understand, without a convicting vision for your life, you will always conclude with a less than life.

Within the last century, the world has changed and evolved into the foggy lens of mediocrity you see on a daily basis. The spark on innovation which caused men to work the twelve hour work day and bring home the leftover energy to give to the family; the movement of women equality and wars, have played a tremendous role in how men ended up so confused and lost. You may be like 82% of the men stuck in "guyland"; where you get a free pass from the world for constantly delaying adulthood. Well, news for you, that's not what you were designed and created for. You were created to LIVE and BE great. You were created to cast value on all lives in your community.[3] You were designed out of love, and created in the image of God. It doesn't get any better than the reassurance of knowing you were created by the most high for a purpose. Knowing that now, what will your story be? Do not let anyone else write your story.

The trail blazed of lifelessness and chaos you see in your rear view mirror is not YOU nor your design. Napoleon Hill said, "Remember, too, that all who succeed in life get off to a bad start, and pass through many heartbreaking struggles before they arrive." After reflecting a little upon your life you should be able to see exactly how you got to where you are now. You should have an answer as to why you are here. In case you missed it, it's to be a fountain and not a drain; to be a life giving spirit and not a life taking spirit. You are here to live a life of abundance in community with those around you.

II. BUILT BY DESIGN

"Remember that you have made me like clay; and will you return me to the dust? Did you not pour me out like milk and curdle me like cheese? You clothed me with skin and flesh, and knit me together with bones and sinews. You have granted me life and steadfast love, and your care has preserved my spirit."
Job 10: 9-12 ESV

The spirit living within you is exactly that - LIVING. Imagine a hammer: it's designed to hit nails. That's what it was created to do. Now, imagine the hammer never gets used. It just sits in the toolbox. The hammer doesn't care. Imagine that same hammer with a soul - a consciousness. Days and days go by with him remaining in the toolbox. He feels funny inside, but he's not sure why. Something is missing, but he doesn't know what it is. Then one day, someone pulls him out of the toolbox and uses him to break some branches for the fireplace. The hammer is exhilarated. Being held; being wielded; hitting the branches - the hammer loves it. At the end of the day, though, he is still unfulfilled. Hitting the branches was fun, but it wasn't enough. Something is still missing.

In the days which follow, he's used often. He reshapes a hubcap, blasts through some sheet rock, and knocks a table leg back into place. Still, he's left unfulfilled. So, he longs for more action. He wants to be used as much as possible to knock things around, to break things, to blast things, even dent things. He figures he just hasn't had enough of these events to satisfy him. More of the same, he believes, is the solution to his lack of fulfillment. Until one day, someone uses him on a nail. Suddenly, the lights come on in his hammer soul. He now understands what he was truly designed for. He was meant to hit nails. All the other things he hit paled in comparison. Now, he knows what his hammer soul was searching for all along.

You were created in God's image; for a relationship with him. Being in that relationship is the only thing that will ultimately satisfy your soul. Until you come to know God, you've had many wonderful experiences, but you haven't hit a nail. You've been used for some noble purposes, but not the one you were ultimately designed for; not the one through which you will find the most fulfillment.[4] Augustine summarized it this way: "You [God] have made us for yourself and our hearts are restless until they find their rest in Thee."

A relationship with God is the only thing that will quench your soul's longing. Jesus Christ said, "I am the bread of life. He who comes to me will never go hungry, and he who believes in me will never be thirsty." Until you come to know God, you are hungry and thirsty in life. You try to "eat" and "drink" all kinds of things to satisfy our hunger and thirst, yet they remain. You are like the hammer. You don't realize what will end the emptiness and lack of fulfillment in your life. Even in the midst of a Nazi prison camp, Corri Ten Boom found God to be wholly satisfying: "The foundation of our happiness was that we knew ourselves hidden with Christ in God. We could have faith in God's love...our Rock who is stronger than the deepest darkness."

Usually, when you keep God out, you try to find fulfillment in something other than God. You can never get enough of that thing. You keep "eating" or "drinking" more and more; erroneously thinking 'more' is the answer to the problem. However, you are never satisfied. Our greatest desire is to know God; to have a relationship with God.

Why? Because that's how you've been designed. Have YOU hit a nail yet?

Knowing and understanding your purpose will allow you to live the most meaningful life possible. David Allan Coe states, "It is not the beauty of a building you should look at; it's the construction of the foundation that will stand the test of time."The foundation of anything must be solid and steadfast. If there is a break or a crack in the foundation, or the anchor isn't properly grounded, there will be instability, and you will drift. The reflection process and looking in the mirror begins today. We want you to take a picture (a before picture) and 31 days from today, we will ask you to take another picture. This will aid you as you physically transform from the inside out. We want you to notate things like: your mood, your attitude, your successes, and your thoughts.

1 Corinthians 6:19-20 English Standard Version (ESV): 19 Or do you not know that your body is a temple of the Holy Spirit within you, whom you have from God? You are not your own, 20 for you were bought with a price. So glorify God in your body.

Being deeply rooted and grounded will allow you to grow exponentially. Your feet do need to be firmly planted on a rock solid foundation in order to propel yourself forward through life. You must be anchored in faith, firmly connected to the intrinsic spirit, and receptive to your surroundings. Your body cannot and will not do anything without your brain telling it what to do. In basic kinesiology - or human movement- the body (structure) has muscles that move after the brain tells it what to do. We have shed a lot of light on your mind as well as your spirit, so now let's connect them to your body.

THE MAKING OF A MAN: TRUE MANHOOD LIES IN THE PROCESS

III. HOW YOU ARRIVED

"Do not be conformed to this world, but be transformed by the renewal of your mind, that by testing you may discern what is the will of God, what is good and acceptable and perfect."
Romans 12:2 ESV

Body-*"So God created man in his own image, in the image of God he created him."*
Genesis 1:27 ESV

So far, you should have had a long look in the mirror, or a chance to lay on your bed and stare at the ceiling in order to reflect on where you are in life. This process should have shown you some of the directional shifts you need to make. We want to make sure we bring you clarity as you continue to grow through life. In the first chapter of Genesis, we see God's creation unfold. In six days he created all that we know. On the sixth day, the "crown jewel" of creation takes place. God created MAN, in his own image to CREATE and CULTIVATE for the intention of MAN to be like HIM. He gave you a mandate to (design, build, generate) as well as to (harvest, nurture, and grow). Men are to be the head of the household in respect to social climate as well as the growth and spiritual climate of the household he represents. Studies show that 63% of youth suicides are from <u>fatherless</u> homes (US Dept. Of Health/Census) – 5 times the average. 90% of all homeless and runaway children are from <u>fatherless</u> homes – 32 times the average. 85% of all children who show behavior disorders come from <u>fatherless</u> homes – 20 times the average (Center for Disease Control). 80% of rapists with anger problems come from <u>fatherless</u> homes –14 times the average (Justice & Behavior, Vol 14, p. 403-26). 71% of all high school dropouts come from <u>fatherless</u> homes – 9 times the average (National Principals Association Report).

You get the point, right? When men don't lead, CHAOS and COLLATERAL damage follows. Men were created to solve problems, not create them. When you are not courageous in aspects of your life, you can be sure there is a path of destruction behind you. What you have to look forward to is a less than desirable future. This all comes from not having a clear perception of what the design is. Since the beginning, men have failed. You all know the story; the first man was a coward and lacked a clear noble vision of the design. I am sure when you were young and heard the story of Adam and Eve, you remember hearing the part of the story when Eve took of the fruit from the tree and saw that it was good for food. If you were like us as a youngster, you hear it's the woman's fault. You think of yourself as this warrior; you say to yourself, "Man if I were Adam, I would never let my wife do that. I would beat that serpent up, or I would destroy that snake. Are you kidding me? If I were Adam, I would use that snake as my belt." Or you may have wondered where Adam was throughout this entire story as it unfolds. Well, let us clear that up for you. Genesis 3:6: "She took of its fruit and ate, and she also gave some to her husband who was with her, and he ate." WOW, talk about failure! Can you see areas in your life right now, where you are a coward, or when you are not aligned with the design? When a man chooses to revere his own will over the will of the natural design and of his family, he becomes a consumer and reverts back to childish tendencies. Look around you or even in the mirror, and see how society has defined manhood. When men chose to act boyishly, they become obsessed with the cheap thrills of life. There are men out there who try to cover themselves up with "good works" or behavior. They try to perform or act their way to good graces. Men like this are generally very proud for the things they don't have or the things they don't do. They often criticize before they even think about following the mandate of design. If you do not have a clear vision or perception of the design, you will be swayed into acting cowardly; you will be a critic. It should be terrifying how easy it is for us men to carry the banner of passivity, mediocrity, and insignificance. Real men, aligned with the design, reject and wage war on all of that.

When you act courageously not even fear can stop you. We have an acronym for fear, it means F-false, E-education, A-appearing, R-real. Remember, what you know has taken you where you are now. You have learned to be comfortable, and for the sake of your growth, you must learn to become uncomfortable. It is time for you to draw a line in the sand, and tell yourself, " I am ready to grow and I refuse to accept anything less than excellence for my life." It is time for you to make a stand and give up childish behavior. You cannot fulfill your design apart from the Creator. Mark today on your calendar as the day you destroy everything in your life that is not excellent. It's time for you to have self-control. "A man without self-control is like a city broken into and left without walls" Proverbs 25:28. It's time for you to align yourself with the design; stand up, show up, and man up.

IV. DEFINING MOMENTS

"He has told you, O man, what is good; and what does the Lord require of you but to do justice, and to love kindness, and to walk humbly with your God?"
Micah 6:8 ESV

Life is a relationship. Going against this concept will isolate you. As a man, you can let fear of failure keep you where you are. Have you ever wanted to speak with your boss about a raise you have been working towards? Perhaps, you have wanted to ask the beautiful woman at the doctor's office out to dinner? Due to fear of rejection or hearing the word "no", you chose to lack courage. Because of your fear, you don't have the raise or the girl. You are experiencing an identity crisis. You know exactly who you want to be and the life you want to live; however, you feel trapped like most men. You feel trapped and isolated in the walls of depression, anxiety, and turmoil. You feel the pressure of not measuring up to anywhere close to what the family expectations of you were. You were voted most likely to be successful in high school, class president, all star athlete, yet, now you are thirty pounds overweight with no self-esteem, no self-control, and buried beyond belief in depression. Maybe you are the guy everyone made fun of, so your soul purpose in life was to get back at everyone who ever doubted you. You chose to live under the bravado of nothing hurts me now, but you are trapped in isolation because you have no intrinsic relationships with anyone. You know everyone but no one knows you.

When you have shallow relationships with everyone and you bank on quantity over quality, you feel truly alone. Can you truly imagine yourself living the rest of your life without being fully known or understood by anyone else?

By design, you were given a WILL. No, not a will of inheritance. A WILL is defined as the burning desire of determination to progress forward. You were given the will to do the right thing, the responsibility to work, and the will to work with the responsibility of a woman. Every man will essentially walk in the shadows of one or two men. They will either walk underneath and carry the banner of the failed; or they will walk underneath and carry the banner of the courageous.

Hopefully, you have started to grasp and understand the focal point. If not, let us be clear here; the focal point is YOU. You are where you are in life, by the choices you have made. Granted, some of those choices were made based on the environment you were in. Ultimately, the choice came down to you. If you are unhappy and dissatisfied with life, you have to look at yourself. You have to look at where your mind is. What are you feeding/investing in it? Look at your heart; what does it beat with? Does it beat with purpose? Is it filled with the yearning or burning desire to make those around you better? Look at your body; it is the only place you have to live. How do you treat it? Do you build it and dedicate time daily to strengthen it? Your mind, body, and heart must be headed in the right direction in order for you to find and dictate success.[5]

If you are like us, you spend the majority of your time between the ages of 10-30 questioning manhood and success. Are you a man when you lose your virginity or a man when you collect your first paycheck? Is manhood defined by turning eighteen, and does the success bell ring when you graduate from high school or college? Are you a man because you got married? Does the world tell you you're successful because you make a six figure income? Are you successful because you have a title at work, and you are stuck on status? Does the world call you a man because you can order a drink at your local bar? All of these things made us question, for a long time, when and what defines successful manhood. We have all been shaped by defining moments, decisions, painful experiences, and personal relationships. It was around twenty-eight when I finally got a clear visual definition of manhood through a connection group at church. It completely transformed my life. That Saturday morning was the defining moment. I found what manhood takes, and what the call to action was. It was not complexed. Honestly, it was exactly how I like things - SIMPLE. I learned manhood was defined as: rejection passivity, accepting responsibility, lead courageously, and invest eternally. We are sure you are saying something similar to what we said, "Wow that's it? This is so simple, yet something no one ever taught us. We clearly were not following this outline throughout our lives. "Let's break this down step by step, and help you evaluate each component. This way, you are clear and concise about how they apply to your life.

- Reject passivity: Since the beginning, mans' default position has been passivity. You were reminded earlier of the story of Creation, and how Adam sat right with Eve as the cosmos were fractured. The ultimate gap was wedged between man and the creator, God. The greatest example of war against passivity is Jesus. He came here - fully man - knowing he had a job to do. His responsibility, by design, was to serve others, lead others to the Father, and DIE for the sins of the world; past, present, and future. That was the ultimate sacrifice and victory over the war against passivity. Look hard, we mean real hard, in the mirror and self-reflect. Pick two main areas in your life where you accept comfort over challenge; you are passive. When we say reject passivity, we don't mean to just turn and pretend it doesn't exist. We mean draw a line in the sand and WAGE WAR against it.

- Accept responsibility: Going back to the fall again. Adam deflected the responsibility to Eve. Actually, if you look closely, he blamed God and Eve. Genesis 3:12," The man said, "The woman whom you gave to be with me, she gave me fruit of the tree and I ate."

Talk about blame shifting. Speaking of which, how often do you blame God or someone else for your life or mistakes? How many times this week have you shaken your fist at someone or even thought to yourself, "Man if this person would just get right, we would be so much better off." Part of being a successful man, is accepting responsibility for where you are in life. The majority of what you do is determined by how you think. As you are reflecting on this chapter, think of two areas in your life where you need to accept some responsibility for your actions. Maybe it is with your wife or children. It could also be with your best friend or even your brother/sister. Look back at the trail you blazed being a coward, and pick one person you burned during that period of your life. Pick up the phone and call them. Tell them you didn't realize how confused you were. You had no idea what you were doing with your life, but you accept full blame and responsibility for….fill in the blank.

- Lead courageously: At the fall, clearly, Adam did not lead courageously. The ultimate model of a courageous leader is Jesus. A leader knows the way, goes the way, and shows the way. A courageous leader provides protection, direction, and life. Looking at your life, do you observe the masses and do the opposite, or do you fall in line and follow the crowd. At your job, how are you leading? With your group of friends, how are you leading? In your household, how are you leading? 70% of youths in state-operated institutions come from fatherless homes – 9 times the average (U.S. Dept. of Justice, Sept. 1988). 85% of all youths in prison come from fatherless homes – 20 times the average (Fulton Co. Georgia, Texas Dept. of Correction). 71% of pregnant teenagers lack a father(U.S. Department of Health and Human Services press release, Friday, March 26, 1999) 75% of adolescent patients in chemical abuse centers come from fatherless homes(Rainbows for all God's Children). Fatherless boys and girls are twice as likely to drop out of high school, twice as likely to end up in jail, four times more likely to need help for emotional or behavioral problems (US D.H.H.S. news release, March 26, 1999). These are some very real statistics of what a lack of courageous leadership does throughout society. Children with involved, loving fathers are significantly more likely to do well in school. They have healthy self-esteem, exhibit empathy and prosocial behavior, and avoid high-risk behaviors such as drug use, truancy, and criminal activity compared to children who have uninvolved fathers. Studies on parent-child relationships and child wellbeing show that fatherly love is an important factor in predicting the social, emotional, and cognitive development of children and young adults. The impact you have on the next generation(s) should be something you think about often. We call it a legacy driven life. As you pierce through your life, look at two areas where your leadership is a must; then, show up.

- Invest eternally: If you do not do what you were created and designed to do, you will never be fulfilled. You may think of how you can do something that leaves a mark for eternity, and we believe it can be summed up with is: how well did you follow Christ, and were you about his glory or your own? In order for you to change the world, you must serve others. When you come home from a hard day's work, do you give your family the leftovers, or do you give them every ounce of love that they deserve from you? Love in itself is sacrificial and selfless. Are you engaged with it? Or do you just throw the word out there and see who grabs it and says it sounds nice coming from your lips? Make all of the moments count, because a life of significance can be born in one single moment. Without a concise definition you are just simply reacting to life as opposed to creating it.

Take time as you do your daily success review, and think long and hard about areas in your life that need immediate attention. Take time to reflect on an area of severe pain, and begin to digest the emotion wrapped around that time. Analyze it, and know that you are now looking at the defining pieces to help you orchestrate a life of success in mind, body, and spirit.

V. YOUR GUT TELLING YOU SOMETHING

"The spirit of man is the lamp of the Lord, searching all his innermost parts."
Proverbs 20:27

Tuck your chin into your chest, and look down. You see that thing between your chest and your belt? What is it telling you? Maybe it's telling you, friend it's time for you to lose me. Maybe it's saying, put food in me now before I am no more. Is it possibly telling you to follow it, because you are about to make a terrible decision? Any way you look at it, your gut is always telling you something. Do you listen when it speaks? When is the last time it told you something, and you didn't listen? Most of us have experienced the sense of knowing something before we know it. Most of the time, we can't explain how we know it. You have the hunch; you go left this time instead of right and bump into your future wife. You have that funny tingle to finally play the lottery and you win. Your body is an amazing structure. It has a wide array of systems that work together to function properly. Your body won't do anything your brain doesn't tell it to do. So many people will tell you not to do this or that. They brainwash you. Well, to be honest, sometimes your brain needs a little washing. You need to get rid of and stop putting JUNK in your brain. Everything you have or don't have is a reflection of who you are; what and how you think, and what you believe in. I am living proof.

Four years ago, I never would have imaged my life could have changed. Up into this point in my life, I was just wandering around confused and trying to replace the empty feeling inside my head with other things. The things would leave me standing still while life was passing me by. I thought I knew what success was. I thought I knew what friendship was. In reality, I was just filling an empty space in between my work days with activities that were just postponing and distracting me from being the person I knew I could be. Talk about ignoring your gut. If my gut told me to go left, I would go right; ignorant and stubborn. If I was truthful to myself, I was scared. I was scared to get to the next point in my life. I was just not ready to reach it. We call this extended adolescence. Before you can make any type of change in your life, first, you must be ready. You must be ready to stand up for yourself and be guided by your instinct. We all have the voice/gut feeling inside our body which points out the correct path to go down. Are you listening to your gut? If your stomach hurts every time you eat Chinese food, then don't eat it! Guess what, your body doesn't like it. If your gut is telling you not to consume another drink, then don't drink it! Guess what, the voice inside your head is foreshadowing a not so good experience. So our question to you is: what are you so afraid of? I am sure there are a few things that just came to the top of your head. Something caused you to get this book. Some event in your life shook the ground from underneath you and made you want to read this book. Your gut told you to keep reading because there is something inside you that wants to improve. Together we are going to discover what that is and help you achieve it.

Eight years ago, after my best friend moved to Denver, my gut told me I would be moving to Denver someday. Throughout the years, I would always find an excuse not to move, and it took me until 4 years ago to find out why. On my last visit to Denver to see my friend, I met my future wife! Up to that point in my life, I always wondered what love would be like. Four years ago, my gut told me now is the time to finally take the leap and go on a new journey. Born and raised on a beach, to now living in the snow over a mile above sea level. Before my journey, people always asked me what if it was not meant to be. My answer was always the same. This is what I am supposed to do. Even if things do not work out the way I am thinking, things are going to work out the way it is meant to be. Life is full of choices. Most of the time, they are easy choices to make. You just have to listen to your gut, and bet on yourself 100% of the time. When you listen to your gut and believe in yourself, you always get taken to the place you are meant to be.

By now, I am sure you have had many flashbacks in your head on many choices you wish you would have made differently. Of course, in hindsight, it is always easy to say," I should have done it differently." Think back to those same choices; to the time you were deciding what to do. Was your gut talking to you? My guess is yes. Now, think of why you ignored your gut instinct. Be honest with yourself. Now, everyone reading this book will have a million different answers, but if you actually think hard about it, they all stem from the same thing - FEAR. It is easy to ignore your gut, because the FEAR inside your head takes over.

VI. MINDSET, HEART SET, HEALTH SET

> *"Now may the God of peace make you holy in every way, and may your whole spirit and soul and body be kept blameless until our Lord Jesus Christ comes again."*
> 1 Thessalonians 5:23 ESV

Our body is what allows us to function daily. It's comprised of organs and cells. It consists of proteins, carbohydrates and fats. Our body contains our nervous system, which includes nerves and the brain. It's through our bodies that we connect to the physical world with our five senses: touch, taste, smell, sight, and hearing.

Your soul/heart is what will determine your personality. It's through your soul, that you live out your relationship with God, the community, and yourself. Your soul likely has three major components – your **mind**, **will** and **emotions**. Your mind essentially has two parts; a conscious part and a subconscious part. So let's break this down. The conscious mind is where you do your thinking and reasoning. This can be called logic. The sub-conscious mind is where you hold your deep beliefs and attitudes. It's also where you have your feelings, emotions and where you retain your memories. Your will is what gives you the ability to make choices. Through a very complexed process, your **mind**, your **will** and your **emotions** are connected to the **body** through your endocrine, nervous and immune systems. The mind and the body are in constant communication with each other. What the mind thinks, perceives, and experiences is sent from the brain to the rest of the body.

Let's take your brain for a ride with a quick perception test from Cambridge University:

Olny srmat poelpe can raed tihs. I cdnuol't blveiee taht I cluod aulaclty uesdnatnrd waht I was rdanieg. The phaonmneal pweor of the hmuan mnid, aoccdrnig to a rscheearch at Cmabrigde Uinervtisy, it deosn't mttaer in waht oredr the ltteers in a wrod are, the olny iprmoatnt tihng is taht the frist and lsat ltteer be in the rghit pclae. The rset can be a taotl mses and you can sitll raed it wouthit a porbelm. Tihs is bcuseae the huamn mnid deos nto raed ervey lteter by istlef, but the wrod as a wlohe. Amzanig huh? And I awlyas tghuhot slpeling was ipmorantt!

Amazing isn't it? You were wonderfully and beautifully made by the Creator, God. The goal is to align all of these critical pieces together to help you bridge the gap between your valleys and the summit. We have discussed your design in great detail. Why you were created" We finally nailed it down and gave you a clear vision/definition of what manhood looks like. We've also given you the model to follow. Now that you have realized where you are, and you have identified areas in your life you can apply the principles to, it's time to get into action mode and do work.

VII. FROM GOOD TO GREAT AND BEYOND

> *"Examine yourselves, to see whether you are in the faith. Test yourselves. Or do you not realize this about yourselves, that Jesus Christ is in you? — unless indeed you fail to meet the test! I hope you will find out that we have not failed the test. But we pray to God that you may not do wrong — not that we may appear to have met the test, but that you may do what is right, though we may seem to have failed."*
> 2 Corinthians 13:5-7 ESV

Life for you might be good right about now. You may have a good job, a good marriage, and you may even have a good body. Do you think you were created for good, or do you think you were created for great? If you are ok with good, doesn't that mean you are complacent? How long are you going to be ok with an average life? It's easy to be average. it's easy to go with the grain. Do you think with the design of man, you were created to just be average? Biologically, because you are a man, we know the answer to that question is no. Every man has an innate nature to be glorious and act as the lion. There is a ferocious ambition to beat your chest after being courageous.

It's time to get off the bench and get into the game. The whistle has blown. As your coaches, we are subbing you in. You were born with every tool necessary to go out and get the job done. Why are you so timid to get into the game? Thought you wanted to play? See, faith and fear both DEMAND you believe in something you can't see. It's your choice as to what you believe in. Where fear and doubt lie, success can't dwell. Fear holds you back from being engaged. Your life is pleading with you to fear not. Have faith in your design, and know you will be tested. It's time to get in the game and fight for a cause. Be intentional about living.

What do you want? Seems like it is an easy question but have you ever thought about it? What do you want to achieve in your life, what goals do you have, what is your passion and the reason you wake up every day? How do you expect to achieve your goals or get to the quote un quote promised land if you have no idea. What makes you happy? What do you like doing? Do you wake up every day excited and pumped up to start your day? A lot of the time, we tend to get discouraged at the place we are at in our life because we expected to be further along and making more money or being more successful, yet we do not even have an idea of who we want to be or where we want to be. This is one of the reasons why so many of us are wandering around feeling empty inside because we are not really sure where we are going or even where we want to be. There is a fire burning inside each and every one of us but you have to spend the time talking to yourself and thinking of what you want in order to achieve it.

Your mind can not commit to achieving anything unless you attach some kind of emotion to your goals which gives you passion. When you create a passion you can achieve anything in this world. This is the key to unlocking your true potential. So let me ask you again…what do you want? The best part of that question is that there is no right or wrong answer. Whatever your answer is you are hundred percent correct. Think about it, believe in it. Have you ever heard the phrase you can do anything that you put your mind too; well it's a correct statement. The key is figuring out what your mind and heart are telling you.

When you find your answer to that question, put some emotion in it, make it your passion to achieve it, then go do it. When you have passion burning inside your heart the sky's the limit.

Living a mission focused life might be difficult for you at this moment in time. You may have been simply drifting through life; just getting by. You may be deemed successful by your peers because you have a decent job, a nice car, and you seemingly can do whatever you want when you want. Well, what is the standard and who set it? If you compare your less than life with your neighbor's less than perfect life, who's winning? You have been called to a life of purpose.

Let's examine the story of King David. He grew up as a farmer's smallest, youngest, and weakest son. He was about fifteen years old when Samuel was told by God, David was who he had chosen to anoint as Israel's next king. From that time, the Spirit of God came upon David, and he began to show signs of coming greatness. He went back to his sheep on the hillsides around Bethlehem. God was with him. David grew up strong and brave; not afraid of the wild beasts which prowled around and tried to carry away his sheep. More than once he fought with lions, and bears. He killed them when they seized the lambs of his flock. David, alone all day, practiced throwing stones in a sling until he could strike exactly the place for which he aimed. When he swung his sling, he knew the stone would go to the very spot he was throwing it. All through the reign of Saul, there was constant war with the Philistines, who lived upon the lowlands west of Israel. When David was still with his sheep, after he had been anointed by Samuel, the camps of the Philistines and the Israelites were set against each other on opposite sides of the valley of Elah. In the army of Israel were the three oldest brothers of David. Every day, a giant came out of the camp of the Philistines, and dared someone to come from the Israelites' camp to fight him. The giant's name was Goliath. I am sure you remember this story from your childhood. He was nine feet tall. He wore armor from head to toe, and carried a spear twice as long and as heavy as any other man could hold. His shield bearer walked before him. He came every day and called out across the valley: That he was the greatest Philistine soldier and that he would fight any contender and if the contender killed him, the Philistines would submit to the Israelites. But no man in the army, not even King Saul, dared to go out and fight with the giant.

For days, the camps stood against each other. The Philistine giant continued his call. One day, David's father Jesse, sent David from Bethlehem to visit his brothers in the army. David came, and spoke to his brothers. While he was there, Goliath came out in front of the camp calling for someone to fight with him. The promise made by King Saul was that if any man will go out and kill Goliath they would receive a great reward, a high rank in the army, as well as his daughter as his wife. David was curious as to who was calling out the army of Israel and his brothers laughed and scolded him for leaving his flock according to the story in 1 Samuel 17. David knew he could stand up to the Philistine that challenged the army. David was taken to King Saul and again was told he was just a boy and too small. David with great courage let the men know he was not ashamed and not afraid to fight and that God would protect him. David was given King Saul's armor but David was used to fighting bears and lions, not men. He was used to knives and slings, not armored helmets, shields, and swords. So he went to fight, with no amour. While everybody in the army had been looking on the giant with fear, David had been thinking out the best way for fighting him; and God had given to David a plan. It was to throw the giant off his guard, by appearing weak and helpless; and while so far away that the giant could not reach him with sword or spear, to strike him down with a weapon which the giant would not expect and would not be prepared for. David took his shepherd's staff in his hand, as though that were to be his weapon. But out of sight, in a bag under his mantle, he had five smooth stones carefully chosen, and a sling, -- the weapon that he knew how to use. Then he came out to meet the Philistine. The giant looked down on the youth and despised him, and laughed. The biggest difference is Goliath fought for men and pride, and David fought for God

So David ran toward the Philistine, as if to fight him with his shepherd's staff. But when he was just near enough for a good aim, he took out his sling, and hurled a stone aimed at the giant's forehead. David's aim was good; the stone struck the Philistine in his forehead. It stunned him, and he fell to the ground.

While the two armies stood wondering, and scarcely knowing what had caused the giant to fall so suddenly, David ran forward, drew out the giant's own sword, and cut off his head. Then the Philistines knew that their great warrior in whom they trusted was dead. They turned to flee to their own land. The Israelites followed after them, and killed them by the thousands; even to the gates of their own city of Gath. So in that day David won a great victory and stood before all the land as the one who had saved his people from their enemies

This story goes to show you a few things. The first thing it shows, is that a king can arise out of the smallest and weakest circumstances. Kingship has its place in manhood.

It reflects a great energy. Kings have strong conviction. They have great moral character and devout leadership. As you grow into manhood, you will where the fabric of a king; as it associates with integrity. This fabric must be worn with care and compassion. Too much fabric at the wrong time and you become a dictator or a tyrant. Too little of this fabric and you will struggle with compromising. Even the alpha male, who seems to have it all together, is probably in some cases just like you. When apart from the spirit, he has no noble vision and lacks courage just as King Saul did. When Saul saw a problem that seemed like a giant (Goliath), he was afraid. He compromised his position as king and leader.[6]

Another fabric you clothe with as a man is the fabric of a warrior. The warrior <u>leads courageously</u>. The warrior takes initiative. He wants to protect, and he has a great deal of perseverance. As you grow into manhood and wear the warrior's fabric, you will fight for what matters most. Again, you must be careful. Too much of this fabric can make you harsh and abusive. Not having enough of this fabric; you will come across as a wimp. Growing from good to great takes a vision for knowing what you are trying to accomplish. You need to anchor down on a solid foundation and begin to walk, step by step. To grow from great to beyond takes a great deal of faith, trust, and obedience.

VIII. THE ARCHITECURE OF YOUR BODY

> *"Rather, speaking the truth in love, we are to grow up in every way into him who is the head, into Christ, 16 from whom the whole body, joined and held together by every joint with which it is equipped, when each part is working properly, makes the body grow so that it builds itself up in love."*
> Ephesians 4:15-16 ESV

The body is wonderfully and carefully made by design. It has a number of working parts and different systems that work together in order to function properly. There is, however, a shelf life. These things were not built to last for eternity. The mission is to live a well lived life and to lead by example in all areas for your family and community. In this segment, you will learn what you need in order to get a head start on how to get a body built for the challenges you will face. We will suit you from head to toe, and prepare you for a life of eternity.

Ephesians 6:10-18: " Finally, be strong in the Lord and in his mighty power. Put on the full armor of God, so that you can take your stand against the devil's schemes. For our struggle is not against flesh and blood, but against the rulers, against the authorities, against the powers of this dark world and against the spiritual forces of evil in the heavenly realms. Therefore put on the full armor of God, so that when the day of evil comes, you may be able to stand your ground, and after you have done everything, to stand. Stand firm then, with the **belt of truth** buckled around your waist, with the **breastplate of righteousness** in place, and with your **feet fitted with the readiness that comes from the gospel of peace**. In addition to all this, take up the **shield of faith**, with which you can extinguish all the flaming arrows of the evil one. Take the **helmet of salvation** and the **sword of the Spirit**, which is the word of God. And pray in the Spirit on all occasions with all kinds of prayers and requests. With this in mind, be alert and always keep on praying for all the Lord's people."

Truth- It keeps you secure. It helps make all of the other pieces effective as it holds everything in place.

Breastplate- A soldier who is equipped and armored with this piece will stand bold in battle with confidence. Without this protection, anything can pierce the heart.

Fitted Feet- This allows you to step freely and without hesitation. They aid you in your movement as well as your defense.

Shield- This not only shields your entire body, but also the rest of your armor. The shield is a constant; no matter which way it is aimed. It moves with the attack.

Helmet- The helmet will protect your mind and your thoughts. It helps prevent any fear or doubt from creeping in.

Sword- This is the only weapon in the armory that can be used for offense or defense. It will not only allow you to strike with no fear, but it is also used a defense. A defense from arguments and lies you can buy into; which will ultimately betray you.

This is not something given to you, or placed on you by someone else. THIS IS YOUR ARMOR. It's up to you to pick it up and put it on. After you put it on, you are commanded to STAND!

Taking care of your body relies heavily on a few basic principles. If mastered, they can lead you to a healthy style of living. "Take care of your body. It's the only place you have to live" (Jim Rohn). The first basic principle to a healthy lifestyle is controlling how much food you eat at a certain period of time. When you eat, it is used as fuel or nourishment to your body. It is meant to supply the body with energy, so it can function properly. In its design, it gives the body the nutrients it needs and an essential dosage of vitamins to perform optimally. If our body does not get the right fuel and nourishment, our basic body functions are inhibited. In that case, our health can decline. In excess, this can be harmful as well. If we eat too much, we become overweight and are subject to developing disease such as diabetes, heart disease, stroke, and cancer. In short, what we eat is central and essential to our overall health. Food acts as medicine to maintain, prevent, and treat diseases. Instead of seeing food as the enemy or villain, start to see it as way to create health and aid the body in natural functions.

IX. WHAT DO YOU SEE WHEN YOU LOOK IN THE MIRROR

> *"When I was a child, I talked like a child, I thought like a child, I reasoned like a child. When I became a man, I put the ways of childhood behind me. 12 For now we see only a reflection as in a mirror; then we shall see face to face. Now I know in part; then I shall know fully, even as I am fully known."*
> 1 Corinthians 13:11-12 ESV

One of the things you cannot avoid is that at some point in the day, you will look in the mirror. Some of us look at it with confidence; while others gaze disgusted. The latter is a product of low self-esteem. We wonder how we let ourselves get this bad. The mentality is weak, the body is flabby, and the spirit is crushed. Have you been there before? Are you there now? When most men see themselves in the mirror, they see a toss between the warriors they are supposed to be - yet aren't -and the man with boyish tendencies that they have yet to escape. Everyone wants to be something, but not everyone has the discipline to become it.

So, tell us what you see....What you see has been determined by courageous moments, hopeless moments, and monumental moments. Every man's central drive stems from events in their lives - which most often than not - they don't understand. The only way for you to look in the mirror and like what you see, is by staring back at the reflection, and figuring out what has molded you.

Have you ever heard of a spirit wound before? They are the deepest wounds any man can experience in life. These particular wounds do not heal. They continue to garnish pain over and over again. Normally, most men deal with these wounds in a very specific way. They pretend the wound isn't there. Any wound left unattended adversely impacts and shapes the dynamic of your life. Where do you find your heart? Does it work in conjunction with your mind and your body? The (mind, body, spirit) connection is necessary for you to optimize the quality of your life. Your body hears everything your mind says.

To exceed your past vision, you must first realize there is a problem. Second, uncover the hole you dug to store all of your problems in. Then, face your problems head on with community. How do you do that? Sometimes we get turned around so much we do not realize how far we have strayed from the goal or vision we created of the person we want to become. Every little step in the wrong direction moves you slowly down the wrong path. You become blinded by how far you have traveled in the wrong direction. With this obstructed view, a powerful shock to your brain may be necessary to show you the truth behind a blurred version of yourself. Because you moved slowly – yet steadily - in the wrong direction it does not seem like you are as far down the wrong path. This causes your brain to send signals which cloud your mind into thinking nothing is wrong. If nothing was wrong, then why do you have that empty feeling inside? This vicious cycle hinders you from truly seeing the person everyone else sees.

It is not a bad thing to have strayed off track. In fact, it gives you the opportunity to tap deep inside of yourself to correct it. Now is the time to take action! When you realize there is a problem, you have to attack it full on. Often, we want to leave our problems buried. We want to forget about them; pretend they didn't happen. In that solution, nothing gets addressed. The real question remains: why are you afraid to face your problems? Are you scared of being alone? Scared of growing up and being the man you are meant to be? Scared of what your "friends" will think. These potential fears - even if they are different than the ones mentioned above - all come from the same source.....You and your confidence! Take control of your confidence. Believe in yourself, that you are meant for better; meant for something more. Remember, you are not alone. We have all been through some struggle or situation in our lives. The only difference between the ones who become successful and happy are the ones who continue to struggle miserably is whether they uncovered the potential deep within themselves to believe they can overcome anything.

The value of decisions depends on the courage it takes to make them. Your immediate decision needs to be to face fear head on, and begin to deal with your less than life. You should now understand why you are here, and what you were created for. We have begun to talk about things that have led you to where you are, currently. Now, we want to encourage you to look in the mirror, and become the warrior you are supposed to see. All of this will be done by peeling back the layers of pain and dealing with it. You must accept responsibility for thinking the thoughts which have led to where you are. So, roll up your sleeves, and deal with some of the intrinsic wounds of the spirit. A rough start does not have to be the final story in a man's life. You are called to be the coauthor of your life. By understanding your past and what you see in the mirror, you become better equipped to stand with God to coauthor your story. I am sure growing up, you heard statements like, "Be a man. Men don't cry." Or," Suck it up, and figure it out." Most of these statements were probably made by men you looked up to, respected, and held in a high regard. You were taught to never be vulnerable, or never show how much you were hurting. How did that work out for you? There must be a time in a man's life where he draws a line to define what was then and what is now. You have to take a stand against the natural rule of passivity and the control it has reigned over your life.

Engaged or passive, absent or present, a "father" serves a monumental and pivotal role in shaping a man's life. Spoiler alert, you were not raised by a perfect dad, and that has left a deep scar on your spirit. Every father gets undeserved admiration from the son, in some degree or another, the second they are born. There is an ongoing battle of emotions and social implications caused by a lack of relationship with fathers. It has to be dealt with at some point. All in all, it's about how your dad related to you. If you are like 33% of children who grow up in a fatherless household, there is a huge hole left in your life. Part of what fills that hole is rage.

You are someone we call a bottler; someone who chooses to pretend like you were not affected by your dad. According to John Sowers in the Fatherless Generation, "Fatherlessness creates an appetite in the soul that DEMANDS fulfillment. " This hunger will come to the surface somehow. It may present itself in the form of addiction or obsessions to drugs, pornography, or even performance. You suffer from a spirit sense of loss or incompleteness. Incompleteness is relational; where you never felt accepted or validated by your dad. Incompleteness is informational. Your dad didn't teach you to tie a tie, or balance life and work, or how to court and properly date a woman. With the help of the spirit, you can overcome anything.

The spirit wound of the father is very deep and sometimes can cut straight through the bone into the depths of the soul. Sometimes, you probably won't realize it is there. You live your life wondering why you could never measure up, or why you were never accepted. Maybe you question why he wasn't around. Those thoughts are manifestations from the hole that needs to be fulfilled.

Mothers also have created wounds which have shaped your life. Her influence molds your view and treatment of women. There needs to be separation from mother at birth, which serves as the physical space in which ties need to be broken. When you transition into manhood - or are called from boyhood/guyland into manhood by another man - there must be an emotional separation from mother. If you are overly connected to your mother, you may feel like your masculinity is threatened. If you have an unhealthy relationship with your mother in the emotional space, it can cause you to feel threatened by women. With this dilemma, you usually travel down two paths: either you are a dominant male or you are a soft, passive male. The mother wound and the impact it has on your life is generally caused by an absent, disengaged father. Mom can sometimes be overbearing as she stands in the gap for the distant father, because she is trying to fulfill the role of mom and dad. If your mother was experiencing her own pain, due to a lost connection with your dad, she will tend to make up for it by over connecting with you.

Understanding these intrinsic spirit wounds is a must. They are the essence of your natural existence, as well as serve as two monumental life shapers. Since you have reflected and observed the roles your mother and father play, it's time to begin the healing process. No longer should you have to carry the burden and pain. You must choose to deal with these wounds in a respectful and responsible way. One of your definitions of manhood is to accept responsibility. Ultimately, the burden of resolving and healing rests in your hands. It is detrimental to your own life story. You must deal with forgiveness first.

You have to decide that there is no longer any punishment needed, and no force to be dealt. Part of the role of the community is to share some of your struggle and pain with, so you can begin to deal with these intrinsic stones you have been carrying your entire life. You have to initiate contact, and realize you cannot control their response. You have to realize it's not important. Identify the exact issues and vocalize them. If you don't heal, you will not be able to fully live in the present. Part of your soul will remain rooted in the past. You may struggle to trust or experience intimacy with a spouse or those who could be close friends. You have a subconscious mind to ruin relationships in order to decrease the risk of being wounded by someone else again. However, a man who has healed is capable of intimacy with close friends and a spouse. You are willing to take on the risk of being vulnerable with others and make yourself fully known. You will be at peace with your past, and able to fully live in the present. You can move boldly and proudly into the future.

When you look in the mirror, there should only be one person in the reflection, and that is YOU. Do you realize no one has hurt you more, lied to you more, or done more damage to you, than you? Seeking your own desire outside of the natural order and going against the design will bring about chaos with severe consequences in your life. When you fall prey to isolation, you are dealing with an enemy way too powerful for you. Your outlook on life is completely perverted. You suffer the pain of making careless mistakes and outrageous choices. Studies show that social isolation kills more people than obesity does. In fact, it is twice as deadly as obesity. It is also more dangerous than lifelong smoking. Living a life of isolation goes completely against the creative design and natural order of the universe. The more and more you draw away from people and the less known you are, the greater chances you have of depression. This leads to a less than happy life. Proverbs 18:1 states, "Whoever isolates himself seeks his own desire; he breaks out against all sound judgment."

The way to solve this was mentioned in the beginning of this book. You need a community of men, and you desperately need a valiant advisor. You need a group of men who can encourage you and stand in the gap for you as you make decisions.[7] Particularly, your advisor can walk in front of you to guide you as to which decisions to make to produce the best outcome for your life, because they care about your success. Choosing an advisor is very important, as you must be careful who you take advice from. For example: In high school, you really wanted to make the varsity basketball team. You thought you had a decent jump shot, you were fairly quick, and you understood the game because you played it throughout your life. Whether it was when you were younger or goofing off in your neighborhood, you were familiar with the game. You can always ask the HEAD COACH, how to make the team. You could even ask some of the players who made the team last year; what are your chances of making the team in order to get an insight on how coach runs practice. You however, should never ever ever ask all the kids who got cut from the team last year or in previous years, how to make the varsity basketball team! Why do you ask? It's because they don't know how. They are not where you want to be at this point. If you want to have a successful marriage, don't ask the person who has been divorced four times. Clearly, they have no clue. You ask the man who has been married for twenty five to thirty years. You want to seek wisdom from people who can set the bar high and not belittle you when you don't reach it. They encourage you, and lift you up. Those are the ones you want to support you while you're reaching for those goals.

Your colleagues or running mates walk through life at the same pace with you. They will love you with everything they have, and they are committed to your best. Let's stick with the same analogy for reference. Let's say you make the team, because of your hard work and skill. You developed these qualities because you took the advice of the head coach and players from the previous year. What do you do when you get what you want? No one on that team, including the coaches, is saying, "Man I sure hope we lose every game this season. We are shooting for mediocrity this year boys." Are you kidding me? Every player on the team wants to hoist a trophy over their heads, and be called "champion". You are all fighting, sweating, and working hard for one common goal; to win every game. Now, will you win every game? It's a possibility. The point is to surround yourself with people who can run the race of life with you; who you can be clear with; and who know you. They are there to celebrate the wins and in the pits for the losses. These men know your faults. They know your weaknesses. They know your strengths, and how to pull the best parts of you out to shine for the world to see.

To nurture these relationships and to personally be a healthy colleague, you have to have some key characteristics. Be loyal and encouraging to them. You have to be fully interested in your running mates' lives. You need to take an interest in who they are, and what they are trying to accomplish. You must also be willing to bare your heart, share your pain and be vulnerable. You must be as the spirit, and lean in or initiate conversations with other men.

X. HEART DETERMINES LIFE

"Above all else, guard your heart, for it is the wellspring of life. "
Proverbs 4:23 ESV

Have you ever started doing really well at life, and then all of a sudden you get hit with the tornado of life? You didn't see it coming, it came without warning, and it serves to wreak havoc on everything you have built up? Take notice, because this will happen as you get accepted into manhood, and you are following your purpose of life. It will attempt to break your spirit. You will be exhausted. You may become discouraged and confused. In the midst of this storm lies an objection. You need to be able to connect with your spirit. Issues with your spirit will affect everything you do. If it is not cared for, your body will rot from the inside out. Every man has issues of the spirit they wrestle with constantly. All of your heart issues affect you at your core. The spirit you have was breathed into you by the creator. Anything that goes against the natural design will weigh on you and wrestle with your spirit.

You have a burning desire, regardless of what stage of life you are in, to create a utopia in your life. You want everything to be perfect. You want a place where you feel no pain; where there is no wrong, and all of your desires are fulfilled. In an attempt to create this place on earth, you go through painful experiences, live in doubt, and become frustrated at you constant failures. There is a day coming where the ultimate warrior king, will return. Revelations 21:4 says, "Wipe away every tear from their eyes, and death shall be no more." Who and what sets the standard for your life? If you look to the millionaire for the standard, you are still looking at an imperfect, broken being. How do we know this? Just watch the news.

Day after day, a famous celebrity is committing suicide. It goes to show, collecting transient things leads to nowhere. It shows you money does not bring you completeness. Does the guy who has the pretty wife and good job set your standard? He lives in secrecy. You have NO idea just how much he hates his life, because all he does it work. Due to the nature of his job, he never sees his beautiful wife, or spends time with his kids. He is longing for an intrinsic relationship with his wife. He wants to be available for his children, yet doesn't have the time. He misses his son's special moments at baseball practice, and his daughters' ballet recitals. He thinks he is doing a fantastic job as a father and husband, because they can pay all their bills and the kids have everything they need. All the while, the wife is feeling disengaged and lonely. So, she seeks attention elsewhere. The kids are constantly performing for the invisible dad. The son grows up thinking being a man is comprised of hard work and nothing else. The daughter has an empty feeling which needs to be fulfilled. Truth be told, she will let anyone fill that void; as long as it makes her happy for the moment. You know that will not sustain, and the cycle will continue to repeat itself. So, we ask you again, who sets the standard for your life? Romans 3:10 explains, "There is no one righteous, not even one." There you have it. The world is busted. People are broken. You can't look for them to create the standard for your life. The answer to your spirit is not morality, religion, psychology, or even self-help. The solution is found in the book of truth, "While we were yet sinners, Christ died for us" (Romans 5:8). Jesus Christ is the standard, and the only solution for walking in oneness with the spirit. Spoiler alert, walking in the spirit does not mean everything in life will be perfect, or that you have your utopia. That tornado is still coming to wreak havoc on your life; trust us. However, you now have the solution, and there is nothing above Him. There is nothing else to gain and nothing else to get. He is enough, and that's great news.

As a man who is not engaged with the spirit, you are set up for failure; which leads you into damaging space. You may be intelligent and headstrong, but if there is no connection to the spirit, being smart doesn't cut it. You simply wake up in the morning, and walk through the motions of life without a noble vision or any heart connection. You stuff all your problems away; at some point those issues start to take up roots and will surface. Most likely, it'll be when you least expect it. Do you just want to survive, or do you want to live?

You must feel feelings. To be honest about what you're feeling, you have to have a harmonic approach. If you are angry, tell someone you are angry. Share deep felt emotion, and begin to dissect it. We all struggle and wrestle with the same things throughout our life journey. We live in a busted world full of broken people. Once you realize everyone struggles and you are not the only one, it takes a lot of weight and pressure off of yourself to perform. Facing the trauma of your spirit alone is impossible. What would happen to you if you didn't know how to swim, but you jumped in the pool? You would probably not be here reading this book right now. You could not save yourself. Something outside of yourself needs to save you.

When you are stuck in your head; in a pattern of analyzing, overthinking and trying suggestive reasoning, you become confused in life. When you can simply tap into your feelings and tune in to your heart's wisdom, you will always find the clarity you are seeking. Look into your heart. Your head energy is driven by your internal programming, your morals, and the identity you have created. Your heart/spirit energy is LIMITLESS - infinite and unrestricted. Your heart/spirit has the ability to completely alter your life if you listen to it. It guides you to greater aliveness, and gives you life to the fullest. This is a distinction we believe men have struggled with for centuries. We feel the common factor is that men are taught to be strong and not show emotion. We directly correlate emotions with heart. If you show emotion, you are weak and fragile. Men are meant and designed to be warriors and rescuers. The problem remains; if a man does not have an intrinsic connection with his heart, he a victim with a super hero persona. Basically, all super heroes attract victims. Therefore, his internal connection has to be changed. Yes you were created to be a warrior, but that warrior imprint came from the spirit. The thoughts of your head flow from your heart. God has written upon the hearts of all humanity the way to fulfillment, and the way to overcome every challenging issue of life. "Keep thy heart with all diligence; for out of it are the issues of life" (Proverbs 4: 23). Keeping your heart with diligence means paying attention to, listening, and connecting with the subtle and consistent impressions of the heart. A heart that has been imprinted with HIS LAW leads to joy.

The Heart determines whether thoughts, words, and deeds will sink or swim! It is the Heart which is foundational and primary; not the Head. Failing to acknowledge the Heart and its rich Biblical meaning, a person might proceed to live like a prideful dryer. They pridefully primp their magnificent clothes drying ability — while failing to acknowledge their own electrical cord and the electricity supplied by a nearby outlet. You see, with no electricity, the dryer has pride in nothing! It is vital to remember that The Heart represents our connection to the Creator. This intrinsic oneness is vastly more important and fundamental than the machinations of the mind alone. "A good man brings good things out of the good stored up in his heart, and an evil man brings evil things out of the evil stored up in his heart. For the mouth speaks what the heart is full of" (Luke 6:45).

This scripture firmly establishes the directional flow of idea initiation while opposing pervasive rhetoric of brain teaching. That directional flow is Heart to Head — not vice versa. If you stubbornly insist it is Head to Heart, such an assumption parallels the logic of the prideful dryer, who fails to acknowledge the source of electricity which makes drying possible in the first place. The importance of this truth has a stunning application: You cannot directly choose to be happy!

Happiness is not something you can create within the cognitive realms of mental will. You can't simply awake one morning (as the popular rhetoric reasons) and say to yourself, "Today, I'm going to be happy!" No, life doesn't work that way. You can no more choose to be happy of your own positive mental will, than a prideful dryer can dry magnificently without being plugged into electricity! Instead, what you can do — just like the prideful dryer should — is humbly acknowledge the electrical source that makes all drying possible. As you acknowledge the source of all Life, Love, and Light the happiness will spontaneously flow to you and through you, without taking any thought to create this happiness via your Head. With the God-given gift of free will, you can choose to attach yourself to the True Vine. As you do, you will grow and flourish according to Divine Design. In contrast, as you fail to attach yourself to the True Vine, you can still dry clothes. You can even boast of your drying . But you cannot do anything of eternal importance, which is part of the natural design and definition of true manhood. Just as you cannot directly change your mind through mental mechanics to be happy, you cannot change your heart through the same device alone." And I will give you a new heart, and a new spirit I will put within you. And I will remove the heart of stone from your flesh and give you a heart of flesh. And I will put my Spirit within you, and cause you to walk in my statutes and be careful to obey my rules" (Ezek. 36: 26-27)."Therefore, if anyone is in Christ, he is a new creation. The old has passed away; behold, the new has come"(2 Cor. 5: 17).

Now, back to the metaphor of the "Heart," and what it means to experience a Change of Heart. The Heart metaphor represents your close connection with the Creator. A lack of closeness is symbolized by a "hard heart." Contrary to the conclusions of the world, if you desire to change the core of your character, you cannot directly do so through feeling-filled visualizations. The example I will use is seeing yourself "as if" you are already a person of higher character, and reinforcing this mental image with the chanting of positive self-affirmations. This is a prideful dryer mentality. It is the erroneous reasoning of "clay" saying to the potter, "thou made me not." Using mind-power only, you cannot bring about a fundamental change to the core of your character. Jesus confirmed this truth by posing a probing question: "And which of you by being anxious can add a single hour to his span of life?"(Matt.6: 27). You can only increase in the stature of your character through Christ—the True Vine. You will experience a change of heart by honoring and obeying the way of the Creator (John 1: 3, 10). Then, He changes the core of your character. He makes you a new creature from the Heart.

Human beings are completely incapable of adding to the stature of their character through will power and emotion-filled, mental imaging. Even a prideful dryer which fails to acknowledge its own electrical cord and the outlet from which it receives electricity, can still dry clothes with the best of them. In a likely manner, by using emotion-filled visualizing techniques, you can accomplish many things: You can become a better bowler and a more dazzling dancer. You can improve your golf swing and your basketball jump shot. You can become more proficient in all outward physical skills. You can also increase the size of your car, the size of your house, and the size of your income. You absolutely cannot change the intrinsic core of your character. The implications of this true conclusion has earthshaking applications.

Changing the intrinsic core of your character is the key to overcoming every annoying habit and addiction that holds you captive. Through the righteous change of heart, all abusive behaviors disappear. All crime comes to an end, and all internal and external battles cease. You plugging in and engaging with the source is what makes this miracle possible. You must first move beyond the mindset that the world is a magic genie to satisfy your desires. You must also understand the real existence of The Creator of the Universe, and tune your heart to be in harmony with His will. The popular assumption that intellect can make all things possible is shattered into a million pieces. The illusion that this power can create anything of eternal importance evaporates. The most significant thing to remember is through Mind power alone you cannot directly change your heart and be joyful. Only the Creator- through his natural design - can make you new. Only He can give you a new heart and spirit. The Creator is the preeminent source of all healing and joy. Only by being obedient to the source and its natural order can you receive the promised blessings of joyful living and fundamental change from your core.

While you can't directly choose to be joyful, you CAN make choices that will result in joy. Joy is the natural consequence that comes as you live in harmony with your own intuitions of truth. Therefore, choosing to be true to the Truth results in joy. The Creator designed mortal life in such a way that when you live true, you know that you are living true. The reinforcing result called "joyfulness" is your possession. Likewise, when you are not full of joy, the Creator intentionally designed the consequences of anxiety and depression. That way, you know you are not living in harmony with His Truth. Thus, being unjoyful causes you to take a personal inventory; "What am I doing that is affecting my life in this manner to this undesirable condition?"

THE MAKING OF A MAN: TRUE MANHOOD LIES IN THE PROCESS

XI. IN SYNC IN THERE

Your personality has three distinct layers - intellect, emotion and action; what you think, what you feel and what you chose to do. Intellect: Your opinions on issues, philosophies on life and attitudes towards yourself and others. Emotion: Your moods, desires and passions; what you love and what you hate, what you are scared of and what attracts you. Action: Not your beliefs or feelings, but what you actually do; how you live your life, and how you spend your time and energy. Ideally, these three distinct facets should be in sync. Your beliefs and ideals should direct your passions and ambitions, which should in turn be translated into your lifestyle. But, often this is not the case. What you know is right doesn't always feel right, and what you feel like doing is not necessarily what you do. You know you should go and help your mom cut the grass, but you feel like staying on the couch watching television. Then suddenly you hear your phone ring and jump up to answer it. You know you shouldn't watch pornography, and you feel guilty about it, but you do it anyway. Your mind tells you that you are in a damaging relationship; your heart is too scared to leave. You act as if everything's fine.

One of life's greatest protests is to try to overcome this mind-heart-body disconnect in order to develop the right attitude in the mind, positive desires in the heart and then to live up to it by doing the right thing.

XII. THE LANGUAGE YOUR BODY SPEAKS

Or do you not know that your body is a temple of the Holy Spirit within you, whom you have from God? You are not your own, [20] for you were bought with a price. So glorify God in your body.
1 Corinthians 6:19-20 ESV[19]

Being deeply rooted and grounded will allow you to grow exponentially. Your feet need to be firmly planted on a rock solid foundation in order to propel yourself forward through life. You must be anchored in faith, firmly connected to the intrinsic spirit, and receptive to your surroundings. Your body cannot and will not do anything without your brain telling it what to do. In basic kinesiology - or human movement- the body (structure), has muscles that move, after the brain tells it what to do. We have shed a lot of light on your mind as well as your spirit, so now let's connect them to your body.

Do you have any idea what your body says to people? From the arch of your eyebrows to the color of your hair. How you comb your hair to how far your eyes are apart from one another. How big your ears and forehead are to the way you sit. The way you stand. The way your arms swing when you walk. The way you talk. The way you stare. Everything your body does or doesn't do, speaks volumes about yourself to people around you.

Think about it, when you see a larger person wearing clothes that are a tad too small for them, what do you think? It could be a number of things. At first glance you might think, "How awful it is; don't they have mirrors in their house? There is no way they are comfortable in that." Then after you see them walk around a little bit, and your judgment radar is beeping to high heavens, you might start to think, "Well they are a pretty confident person in their own skin." Jealousy might even sink in at that point, because you are not as secure with yourself. All in all, that person's body spoke to you. Let's chat about what your body says to others. Not all of us can be a strapping 6'0 foot, manly man, who looks like they lift small buildings in their spare time. Not all of us have washboard abs and a body that women gaze over as their prized possession. Bodies like that take hard work, dedication, and frankly maybe 20% or less men have bodies like that. Contrary to what you see on TV and in movies, that is not the norm. 70% of men are clinically obese based on KCMU analysis of the Centers for Disease Control and Prevention (CDC)'s Behavioral Risk Factor Surveillance System (BRFSS) 2013 Survey Results. WOW, we said 70%. How alarming is that? Where do you fit in?

Obesity has a tremendous impact on all aspects of your life. A number of studies suggest putting on the pounds not only transforms your belly, but it also alters your brain. These brain changes may fuel overeating, leading to a vicious cycle which makes losing weight and keeping it off challenging. Obesity causes food 'addiction'. Research shows that gaining weight may desensitize the brain to the pleasure we get from sugary and fatty foods. This prompts us to eat more cookies and cake than we did when we were leaner. A similar effect is seen in drug users who eventually require more cocaine or heroin in order to achieve their original high. Obesity may make us more impulsive. In obese men, a region of the brain in charge of controlling impulsiveness, called the orbitofrontal cortex, appears to be shrunken when compared with that of lean men. Obesity is known to cause changes to the immune system; boosting inflammation in the body. This increased inflammation may impact the brain and "lead to a vicious cycle, where the obesity leads to inflammation, which damages certain parts of the brain, which in turn leads to more uninhibited eating and more obesity," according to researcher Dr. Antonio Convit, of the New York University School of Medicine. Obesity raises the risk of dementia. Researchers speculate that the extra fat triggers inflammation, which puts stress on the body and perhaps impacts the brain. The finding suggests belly fat, also known as visceral fat - located between organs in the abdominal cavity, may play a role in reducing brain size. Visceral fat releases a unique profile of hormones which may impact the body in a manner different from the hormones released by subcutaneous fat - or fat under the skin. Previous studies have found that people with smaller brain volumes are at a higher risk for dementia. They also tend to do poorer on cognitive tests. So, not taking care of the only place you have to live will have a long lasting and detrimental impact on every aspect of your life.

We don't expect you to go from 0-1,000. However, we do believe you need to have the presence of mind, a kindred spirit, and a solid body. We are sure you have heard the term, "dress for success", or "dress for the job you want, not the job you have." At the end of the day, we know all men have a self-conscious mind to want to look their best with or without clothes. So, let's dive into making you look the best inside your clothes and out. Today marks the day you are no longer a couch potato. Today is the day you realize your potential and what your body is capable of. Getting your body in line and in tune with your heart and your mind will take some time. Let's begin with what and where you are right now. Whether your goal is to lose weight, get healthy, or maybe just push yourself to new limits, you will accomplish that goal by the end of this book. Scientifically, it takes roughly 66 days to develop a new habit. The goal is to break your bad habits and help you develop new habits that with a lasting effect in your life. It is always about self-reflection, so today, look at where you are physically, mentally, and spiritually. The best part about today is that you do not belong where you currently are. Your growth started the moment you decided to pick up this book, and it will continue long after you put this book down.

How often do you start working out with every intention of transforming your body, only to quit before reaching the midpoint of your goal? Don't worry, you're not alone. Astoundingly, the overwhelming majority of people fail to follow through on fitness goals. There is the initial excitement and urgency, but somewhere along the way we lose sight of the work ethic needed to reach our goals. The main thing to know is that consistency is key. Unfortunately, most people are consistent at being inconsistent. We lack the tools to hit every stride along the path to achieving our goals. Here are a few steps to achieve and maintain positive consistency.

Have a written plan: Habakkuk 2:2 says, "Write the vision; make it plain"

Writing out your visions will allow you to see the plan from the beginning to the end. It may start out bare, but you can fill in the blanks as you go along. The important thing is that it has some structure. You can start with when and where you will be training. Next, and just as important, write down what and when you are eating. Write down which days you will measure and weigh yourself. This should only happen once a week, same day and same time each week. Your plan should be easily accessible so using Google and Apple calendars are a great tool to schedule and log weigh-ins/measurements.

Set realistic expectations.

Many of us have trouble staying on a consistent track towards our goals, because we cannot live up to the expectations we set for ourselves. Create several short term goals in conjunction with your overall final goal. These small victories are important for our psyche. Breaking up your 30lb. overall goal into 5lb. increments creates excitement and happiness 6 different times. Healthy weight loss averages out to about 1-2 lbs per week. You may have ebbs and flows, but this is the standard that you follow. Training 3-4 times a week is sufficient. Your rest days are important because your body needs time to rebuild itself. Tearing down torn muscles will only result in possible injury in the future.

Food expectations may be the hardest, but they are the most profitable. Think positive! If you understand that you are changing your lifestyle for the better and not punishing yourself, this transition will be easier. Make sure you reward yourself. No one likes all work and no play. You've worked hard for 6.5 days, you've earned that reward meal or two.

Find an accountability partner(s).

Once you set your goal, tell someone. This is not about having someone know your every step; it's about having someone who can help you become accountable for the things you have said you are going to do. The person you choose must be someone you trust and don't mind receiving constructive criticism from. You have to understand that trials will come. There will be moments when you want to stay home, eat anything, or just quit. Sometimes you just need the encouraging words from someone else. This person usually knows how to put things into perspective for you. This is why you value this person and must keep them in your corner.

See yourself succeeding

The goal is to put ourselves in the best position to succeed. In order to do this, you must see yourself succeeding. Imagine how you will look once you've followed through on your goals. Know that every completed push-up, every dessert passed on, and every milestone completed moves you a step closer to the success you've envisioned.

When you flip through the pages of the dictionary and look up the word, "fitness", you might be extremely surprised at what you find. Webster's defines it as, "the quality or state of being fit." It is listed as a synonym for health. Health is the synonym for fitness; they mean the same thing. "Why are you pointing this out?" You might ask. It seems that we associate fitness with being skinny and looking a certain way. Being fit for many of us means being smaller/leaner or having bigger muscles. This is not what fitness is at all. Being fit means that your body is in good condition; it refers to the total condition and state of your entire body.

Your reason for living a healthy lifestyle should not be simply to look a certain way. Being fit means that your body is in good condition. As simple as this may seem, it's pretty profound in our society where people are working out every day with no motivation other than to be the size they were in high school or to look like some model they saw in a magazine. They dream of being the guy every girl wants to be with. In no way, shape, form, or fashion are we saying that you should not have goals. We all should have goals and strive to be better in every area of our lives. What we are saying is your reason for living a healthy lifestyle should not be simply to look a certain way; as if you were carved out of brick, concrete, and other precious material.

When this is your only motivation you can become vulnerable to trying just about any and everything to reach that goal. Whether it's limiting your caloric intake to 1100 calories per day, exercising like crazy or taking millions of supplements, none of these activities promotes good health. They promote the external benefits of good health. While you may look good on the outside, your body is suffering internally. Internal suffering will inevitably surface. What's the point in spending money and wasting time on living healthy if you still become sick from not taking care of your whole self?

Living in a health with only an external focus is something we call, "transient training." It's a false form of fitness that is generally very short lived. Fitness with a worldly focus will not benefit any human being for eternity. 2 Corinthians 4:18 ESV says, "As we look not to the things that are seen but to the things that are unseen. For the things that are seen are transient, but the things that are unseen are eternal." The things that we can see are the worldly things. Often, we cherish them above the heavenly pursuits. 1 John 2:17 NLT says, "And the world is passing away along with its desires, but whoever does the will of God abides forever."

The sometimes rabid approach and burning desire to be of a certain physique, and the practice of accomplishing that goal is temporary. Focusing on the external elements is not the entirety fitness. In its entirety, it includes the physical; internal and external, and spiritual man. 1 Timothy 4:8 says, "For while bodily training is of some value, godliness is of value in every way, as it holds promise for the present life and also for the life to come." This scripture will help you understand that while exercising is important, the most important thing is for you to live a life that is godly and that glorifies God.

Have you ever looked at some of the most incredible machinery inventions in this world? Take something as simple as a car. When you need to get somewhere it starts and drives to your destination 99.99% of the time. I was always taught to get oil changes every 3,000 miles or at least once every 3 months, but why? I am no mechanic, but my hypothesis would be: if you take care of something - even by doing something so basic - it could improve the life of your automobile and decrease the chances of some common wear and tear. Now, can things still not run perfectly with your car if you do this? Yes, but again, changing your oil regularly can make a huge difference.

Now, let's examine your body. It is the most amazing miracle known to man. Stop and take a few minutes to think about what an amazing piece of wonder your own body is. You breathe in oxygen and exhale carbon dioxide. Did someone teach you how to manufacture this process? No. From the first second you were born you were able to breathe. When you get cut, your body can heal itself. When you start to overheat, your body starts to cool itself down. Through the power of touch you can connect with another human being. We take it for granted, abuse it, and neglect it.

If we go back to the automobile comparison, if you did not get regular oil changes what would happen? If you did not put the right gasoline in your car, what would happen? My guess is your car will still run but the question is how well will it run and for how long? The same principle relates to your body, however, you cannot trade one in for a better model. You are stuck with one body for the rest of your life. The good news is, you can control how great and smooth it runs no matter what state it is currently in. This makes physical fitness is one of the most talked about topics in the world but the problem is that nobody's ever taught how to manage your own body.

There are a few people out there who took the initiative to seek the information; learn it, and then applied it. I know I was never taught how to do this effectively, so at the age of 23 I went on a quest. I found the information out on my own, but it was hard. Going to the gym for the first time was a nerve wrecking experience. Guys twice my size were lifting tons of weight. People were sprinting on the spinning bikes, and some were running like they were being chased. Talk about being scared. I am sure most of you reading this book can relate to the above statements. The problem in this book is underlined by one thing…FEAR. The fear of trying something new from the ground floor; the fear of how I look compared to the other members in the gym; the fear of being so far behind that the weight of the world is pressing down on you.

If you peel back the layers, "FEAR," is only comprised of lack of knowledge. In the words of John F. Kennedy, "In a time of turbulence and change, it is more true than ever that knowledge is power." Most people do not start, or if they start, they are unable to reach their fitness goals, because they do not know how to reach them. They do not know the right exercises, the right diet, or even where to begin. That is where we come into play. There are many steps you can take to start your fitness journey and gain the knowledge to feel comfortable at the gym or wherever you want to accomplish your fitness goals.

The first step is to write down your fitness goals. For me, it was to be bigger, stronger, and faster; which is still the case today. When I turned 30 last year, I vowed to myself to be bigger, stronger, faster, and leaner than I was in my 20's. Your goals could vary, but you have to discover what they are so you know where to begin. During this book, regardless of your area of personal development you are exploring (example: mind, body, spirit, community) the same principles apply. To get to point B you have to know where you are at today.

After you have your fitness goals, the next step is to develop a plan to reach them. You can research this online, get a personal trainer or ask friends that have accomplished similar goals to give you some pointers. A basic healthy blueprint will consist of a lifestyle (what and how you eat), supplements, and exercise. After you have your blueprint to reach your goals, the next part is to follow them.

I was in the grocery store a few years ago with my personal trainer - who happens to be my best friend. When we got in the checkout line, one of his other clients was in front of us. She had all her stuff on the rubber conveyer belt as did I. Our things were separated by a little plastic divider. On my half of the line was chicken breast, green peppers, lettuce, 96/4 ground beef, a loaf of whole wheat bread, a 32 pack of 20oz water bottles, and 1-1/2 pounds of turkey lunch meat. On her side of the line was a 12 pack of beer, a pack of chicken wings from the deli, 2 bags of Lays potato chips, a gallon of ice cream, and a bag of M&Ms. My trainer took out his mobile phone to take a picture and said out loud. "Good client, Bad client!" Garbage in equals' garbage out. This goes for everything in your life. If you put garbage in your body, garbage comes out. If you put garbage in your mind, garbage comes out.

The point of my story is to show that having a plan and goals are great but you have to stick to them no matter what everyone else is doing; no matter the FEAR you have inside of you trying to prevent yourself from reaching your goals. You do not have to be perfect, but you have to be disciplined enough to stay on track. When you have a fitness or diet schedule, follow it.

As mentioned above, the basic blueprint will consist of a diet, whether you are trying to lose weight, gain muscle, or get lean, a diet is one of the most important factors in everyone's fitness goals blueprint. Your caloric intake (calories consumed) and caloric burn (calories burned) will play a big role in being able to reach your goals. If you are trying to lose weight you need to burn more calories a day than you consume, but still provide your body the nutrients you need to function healthily. If you are trying to gain weight or muscle, you need to eat more calories a day then you burn and provide it the necessary nutrients to do this as well.

One of the most common phrases I heard growing up was "you are what you eat." I never really put too much thought into that phrase until I got older and understood it. You put food into your body, then your body processes it and takes out the nutrients that enable your body to function. It disposes the rest. So, it makes perfect sense that "you are what you eat." Have you ever eaten half of a pizza by yourself and then felt awful? Your body hating you but also your mind for letting you consume that greasy food. Consider the same time you consumed a healthy portion of a grilled chicken breast with some broccoli. My guess is you did not think you liked it as much as a half of an awesome tasting pizza, but I am sure your body did. Reflect on the feeling your body and mind displayed to you after the healthy meal.

Your body is a fascinating machine which does so much more than just let you move around. It communicates with you. As I mentioned above, it will let you know how it feels after the food you consume, but it communicates in other ways. It tells you when you're cold, hungry, and tired. Most of the time when you are "hungry," you really aren't. Your mind is bored and playing a trick on you. The next couple times this happens sit there and listen to your body. Is your stomach growling or is your brain telling you that you're hungry? In other words, listen see where the hunger is coming from. A good example of this is when you are so busy that you don't have time to eat. Most of the time it does not even cross your mind that you are hungry until your stomach starts making noises.

Let's explore another quest. The next time you're eating, slow down and enjoy your food. Do not eat in front of the TV; eat at the dining room table. Eat slower than usual and pay attention to your body. Listen for when it is full. We've all experienced reaching for one more piece of pizza then calling out, " I probably shouldn't do this but I am going to anyway." Your body tells you not to, and you ignore it. Afterward, your body alerts you by upsetting your stomach and making you feel awful. This is a prime example of how your body communicates daily. Since you are aware, the next step is to listen, and you do this by creating a good healthy diet. A diet doesn't mean starve yourself. It means putting in the right resources to keep you running at optimum speed. To go back to the automobile analogy, it's equivalent to having a well-tuned vehicle with the right fuel in it.

The next part of your blueprint can still fall under diet but is supplementation. Supplementation is putting the right vitamins and minerals in your body. I grew up in a house that loved taking vitamins. My parents were convinced popping 30 different multi-vitamins would keep them running perfectly tuned. Well, this is not the case. Certain vitamins you can have more of, like the B vitamins, because they are water soluble. This means your body will take what it needs and discharge the rest through using the facilities. You could have 2000% of your daily value and it probably will not do any harm. Other vitamins, like vitamin A, your body can not process a lot of it. If you had 2000% of your daily value of vitamin A, it would put extra work on your liver and actually do harm to your body. Most of the time, just a daily vitamin is all you need to give your body the nutrients it might not get from your dietary lifestyle. It is always recommended to talk to a nutritionist, doctor, or trainer in order to make the right recommendation based on your body's needs.

The final part in your blueprint should consist of good exercise. Exercise plays a big role in having a healthy body. It clears the mind, reduces stress, and burns calories (consisting of fat, carbs, and muscle). When you exercise, your body will burn calories to give you the energy to move, walk, run, lift things, etc. Your exercise is burning the food you put into your body; the fat you have stored, or the carbohydrates you have in your body gives you the energy to exercise. The type of exercise you do will help you accomplish your goals. For example, if you are trying to build bigger muscles, you want to lift heavy weight so your muscle tears and rebuild stronger. If you want to get lean muscle, you would want to lift a little lighter weight and do more repetitions of your exercise. These are just a couple of examples. My recommendation would be to research what would work best to accomplish your goals or hire a personal trainer.

Why have a healthy body? When I worked at a gym for 6 months in between my gap between college and the start of my business career, I would see a lot of people come through the big red doors looking to join. I was lucky enough to have the opportunity to listen to their goals, show them the gym, and then finally set them up with an investment for their health. Besides helping people join the gym and start reaching their fitness goals, my job also consisted of canceling memberships. This gave me the chance to see both sides of the coin. Let's start with getting people to join.

I know a lot about the FEAR of going to a gym for two reasons. One, I mentioned above with my own personal story of how intimidating it was for me to enter a muscle bound jungle gym for the first time, and get over my own FEARs. The second is because I got to hear so many people's FEARs of joining a fitness club. One thing registered through all the personal stories I heard; if you cannot take care of yourself, how are you supposed to take care of a significant other or family? If you are in and out of the hospital with illness, how is that being a loving husband or a role model for your kids? I am not suggesting you spend 6 hours a day exercising. I am just making a point that as the leader of your household, you have to lead by example.

As the role model for your kids, setting a good example is going to be one of your main goals. Do you want to be the dad that can run around with your kids? Be able to attend every school function? Live long enough to see them get married? If you had a heart attack tomorrow, are your wife and kids going to be able to survive and pay all the bills? Is a gym membership that is $25 a month more expensive than a $200,000 hospital bill you will have to take out of your kid's college fund to pay? The point of this elaborate rant is to demonstrate that by taking care of your body you can not only set a good example for your own kids to implement, but also potentially eliminate this future FEAR.

Many people would not even begin their journey to live a healthier life due to fear of starting, yet, they have never done it before. Perhaps they quit, because they do not know what they are doing. Without a clear workout schedule, they either neglect the gym all together or they come and just walk around, because they do not know what to do. Sticking to your blueprint and reaching out to make a schedule will keep you on track. We believe in you! You just have to believe in yourself. I promise, all of the doors of this world will open up for you. Having your body be in prime condition to line up with your spirit and mind will open your eyes to a whole new world; a world that will show you your purpose in it, and will love you for it.

The blueprint has been laid out for you, now you have to seek the tools to help you accomplish it. One of the best things about living a healthier lifestyle and making a commitment to improving your body is the network of people you surround yourself with. When you walk into the gym what do you see? You see a whole bunch of people with similar goals and ambitions. You see the couple walking on the treadmill at an 8% incline and sweating to lose a few pounds, the guy bench pressing big weights, people laughing, sweating, and pushing themselves to the maximum! That is one of the greatest powers of the fitness community. You surround yourself with people who are striving to live a healthier life and reaching the goals that they set for themselves. There is no judging; just people trying to accomplish their fitness goals. I have met some of the nicest people inside this fitness community. People run 5Ks and 10K races to help a special cause. What a great place to put yourself into. We have preached to you about the importance of surrounding yourself with the right crowd and I cannot think of a better situation to put yourself into then waking up early on a Saturday or Sunday morning to walk or run an event for charity. Not waking up on your friend's couch on Sunday morning wondering what happened last night, how much money you wasted, or how much time you wasted not making a difference in this society.

When you begin looking around, you'll see how everything is connected. The above example is a prime body, mind, and spirit interaction. For me, fitness is a way of piecing my life together. A few years ago I had the pleasure of mentoring a young man who ended up becoming one of my best friends. He was a few years younger - at a strapping 18 years old – when I met him playing roller hockey. One day he came to me broken when his first girlfriend of 2 years broke up with him. Lost and confused, he sought guidance and ended up hanging out. I invited him to work out with me one day. We had a great hour plus of working out and talking, burning calories but also developing a better relationship. Even though he had a free membership to the university's gym, he decided to pay 40 dollars a month to have an opportunity to work out with me. After a few weeks of working out together and building a good relationship, he asked me to mentor him. Honestly, I was not ready for this role at this point in my life, but I accepted the job and took it seriously. I was not the perfect mentor, but I tried my hardest to do the best job I could. I knew how important it was for someone to step into this role at this point in his development. During this time I added 20 lbs of muscle to him. I tell you this, not to brag, but to show you the start to his journey. This small achievement played a gigantic role in his life. It helped him developed confidence. Reaching a goal in an area where you are not strong is huge. That confidence laid the foundation for the heart and soul of his development. He got over his ex-girlfriend, and more importantly, he discovered who he was. From there, he also figured out what he wanted out of life. He went on to join a fraternity and make the roller hockey team for the University. Eventually, he worked his way up to the first line. After college, he graduated with honors. He is currently working in one of the biggest companies in America. He also just moved into an apartment with his girlfriend of 2 years.

The point of this story was to show you the powerful role the body plays in your life. It connects and clears your mind. It opens up an opportunity to be more social and surround yourself with some great people. In my story, the most important part wasn't that I got to work out with him for an hour a day; it was the relationship we built together. I cared about him and his success as a person. That relationship opened up his spirit to some good influence. Sometimes, when I am out selling and I close a deal, I feel like I get lucky. My old mentor taught me that as long as you're out there working hard and doing the right things, usually good things get attracted to you.

You have an opportunity every day to impact and change your own life. To choose the right door to walk through, make the right decisions. You do not have to be afraid. We all have made bad choices before and gone the wrong way. You can change that today. You can start living your life to your fullest, and the best part is we are here to help you. We have been there and there is a community of men around you that can support you, and in return, you can support them. That is what this book is about; working together to all be the men we were supposed to be before we got lost. Now you are found!

XIII. YOUR INFLUENCE MEANS EVERYTHING

You can count the number of seeds in one apple, but you can't count how many apples come from one seed.[8] You, by design, have influence. You chose whether that is a positive influence or a negative influence. Again, are you a fountain or a drain? The greatest leaders lead with the "follow me, I'm right behind you" mentality. It's easy to have the greatest outlook when you already know the outcome.

You like most men, are probably a sports fan. In fact based on CNN/*USA Today*/Gallup poll, 75% of men consider themselves sports fans. Now, in today's culture, we have this amazing tool that freezes time essentially, well just on the TV, called a DVR. This tool allows you to stop, pause, rewind, and rewatch your favorite games. If your favorite sport to watch is college football, you know your team more often than not, plays its games on Saturday night. Now, you have a regular scheduled date night, or possibly even church to attend, maybe a job that forces you to work weekends, or something that doesn't allow you to watch the game. You come home tired and go to bed. By the time you wake up the next morning, or afternoon, depending on what type of night you had, you more than likely already know if your team won or lost. You still want to watch the game…so you grab your favorite snack, fly your team's colors, and hit watch previous show on the remote control to the DVR.

Since you know the outcome, even if your team is down 21 points with 3 minutes to go in the fourth quarter/half…are you nervous? Are you sweating buckets and worrying about what play call is coming in? You probably aren't the least bit concerned with the turnover that just happened, or the terrible officiating. You are NOWHERE NEAR as anxious as you would be had you seen the game 24 hours before in live action. Nope, you are chilled, relaxed and able to enjoy everything going, with no worry in the world, because you already know the outcome. What if you didn't know the outcome? You would be on pins and needles, thinking everything that goes wrong you have the answers to fix it. You have the right play call, the right strategy to control the ball, and everything your coach does and gets paid millions to do……..is wrong and you know better. Have you ever been there? When you don't know what is just above the skyline for you, you are always on pins and needles. You feel uneasy; you can't fully understand why things are going the way they are; you don't fully grasp why your life is going left when you tried to maneuver it right. When your outcome is not in your hands and you have no control, how do you feel?

When you already know the outcome, how much more control do you feel you have over whatever situation you find yourself in? If you knew the exact outcome of your life 5 years from now, would you be worried about choices and chances you make today? If your fortune cookie was true, and read "in 5 years you will be a billionaire and all your dreams after that will come true", how would you live your life in the moment, knowing that is on the horizon for you?

The fact of the matter is, men are masters of their domain. You probably don't even ask for directions when you are lost. Men are reluctant to subject themselves to anything that takes control away from them. Men don't like to feel vulnerable. You are supposed to be tough and never show any pain. Honestly, when a man loses control or he feels controlled or captive by thoughts or even other people, it brings back harsh memories of your childhood, when you were told to do whatever just because of your parents. A lack of control to a man is like free falling from the sky, you have no idea where you will land or what you will hit on the way down.

When it comes to this influence, remember you where the fabric of a leader (king) as well as the fabric of a fighter (warrior), but you also where the fabric of someone who can be tender, gentle, and emotionally available; the fabric of a lover. In this make up, you must reflect the fact that you can be vulnerable and emotionally connected to those you are influencing. If you are too emotional, you can be very critical and seem cold, calloused, and isolated. You may also be very over-dependent on those around you, which will put an undue pressure on them they cannot bare. The last fabric of multidimensional manhood is the cloth of a companion. This is solely in the capacity of your ability to converse and connect with other men. Can you be accountable? Can you be encouraging? Can you see one of your brethren struggling and give them a hand up? This cloth is synonymous with a sports team or even your department at work. You are working towards a common goal and without each other the goal is unobtainable. John Maxwell says, "You have to find common ground, and then take the other person to high ground." Meaning you must constantly be uplifting and encouraging as well as (we)centric. When you wear this fabric too much, you become too needy and all your needs must be met and you never give anything. You are a person whose account must always be full but those accounts around you remain in the deficit. When you aren't connected you are obviously disconnected, you are lonely, and that is dangerous.

This fabric is very important as you grow into the man you were created for. You can't influence your community without being able to understand your community. You can't influence your family if you can't connect with your family or even encourage your family. You can't partake in a friendship if you deplete and deflate their existence. You must be multidimensional and be able to wear the different fabrics and have them intertwine with each other and fabric supports one another.

XIV. WHAT LIES BENEATH

The problem is not what exists above ground. The real trouble is lies beneath the surface. Some men get tossed every which way by the winds. You are emotionally broken, physically exhausted, and spiritually depleted. When things happen in your life because you aren't rooted and planted firm/anchored, you are blown in all directions and get beaten up. When storms come, you lose your bearings. When temptation comes, you are led by any and everything. When false teachings cross your path, you are confused. When life doesn't go your way, you are at wits end.

There are teachings that tell the story of another way of living. It tells of strong men who are steadfast, anchored, and immovable. They are fierce and courageous in times of trial and joyful even in hardship. They draw a line in the sand and hold their ground when life knocks them around. WE NEED MORE OF THESE TYPES OF MEN. God didn't design you to be tossed around like a ragdoll and get blown away every time the wind changes direction. You were created and designed for deep connection to Jesus that anchors you and causes you to flourish. But it's not what happens on the surface that makes you strong. It's what happens inside at the core that makes all the difference. "Those who trust in the Lord are like Mt. Zion, which cannot be moved, but abides forever. As the mountains surround Jerusalem, so the Lord surrounds His people from this time forth and forever." Psalm 125:1. God alone is enough to tackle any task and conquer all.

When we seek something in an earnest manner, it is because we believe that it is of great value. Think about all of the things you hold valuable in your life. It could be grades in school to make the dean's list, or the girl you are currently dating or married to; maybe your dream car or house. Your well-being and your joy is directly proportioned or connected to that valuable thing to you. IT SHOULDN'T BE. You should be dependent on God. You are going to have to do some serious work to get to a point where you are earnestly and aggressively seeking a connection with God.

The wrong approach or the white knuckle approach will exhaust you without looking into the core issue.

Many men focus on the exterior part of life and avoid every internal spectrum of the heart. You try to increase your activity level to solve your problems. You work very hard at reading the bible cover to cover, limit your club/partying, spending more time with loved ones, and trying to control all the negative things in their lives. All these things are great things, even necessary things, but they are not the prefix. You have to seek God. "God did this so that they would seek him and perhaps reach out for him and find him, though he is not far from any one of us. 'For in him we live and move and have our being.' As some of your own poets have said, 'We are his offspring.'" (Acts 17:27-28).

God has set the boundaries for where we live in order that we would seek after Him. His will is that every single human being (no matter where they live) would look around their environment and recognize their need for the Lord. The God-void within each of us compels us to want to seek after Him.

Do you get the sense that Jesus is preeminent? That he is top domain with nothing is above him, nothing else to gain or nothing else to get, he is the goal and what life is all about. When you deeply look at these verses you can see how everything in our spiritual pursuit is connected and fixated on Jesus. The way you receive Jesus has nothing to do with how awesome you think you are, or how broken you may be. It is a free gift of grace that you receive through faith. You are a sinner, but in him you have been called righteous. You alone, are incomplete, but with Jesus you have been made whole. You were headed for an eternity of death, but through Jesus you have eternal life. Before him, you were in total darkness and blind, but through him you were brought into the light. You were lost and in exile doomed for the pits of hell, but in Jesus you have been freed. You were once on the outside looking in, but with him you have a seat at the table. Before Jesus, you were the antagonist - the villain. Through Jesus Christ, you have been made an adopted son of the reigning king.

Some of you reading this have suffered catastrophic damage at the hands of a religious institution. They tried to fix you up, change some of the parts on the exterior front, but they completely left your heart alone and unattended. They tried to persuade you to accept their teaching. They told you how to dress, how to talk and even how to think; however none of that has the power to change your core, your heart. What gives you new life is not your deeds or your knowledge and how well you follow instructions. You could be the strongest minded person you know and can will yourself to do anything, but that's not enough; you still need a Savior.

The gospel of Jesus says that through hurt, wounds, and scars and brokenness of your heart run more intrinsic than you ever realized, the grace of Jesus is vast and stronger than you ever imagined. No matter what type of grime, junk, dirt, filth, and darkness you find in your heart when you look deep in there and search; Jesus is neither surprised nor worried about what is in there. He can handle all your sins. In Him, you can live with joy no matter what fault lines run through your heart.

If you want to avoid blowing in the wind, you must anchor your life in the gospel of Jesus Christ. As a spiritually sound and anchored man, you must develop a gospel root system in your heart so deep and so soiled that nothing can blow you around. You must grow and expand roots of prayerfulness so you can enjoy friendship with Jesus more and more. You must grow in service so you have a genuine love for people that Jesus loves. You must be obedient so your desires are no longer burning for things that don't complete you. You must grow roots of worship so your heart's yearning affections are just for Jesus.

Gospel roots provide nourishment and strength so that you are built up to maturity and are established in the faith. This kind of life transformation does not happen because of what is inside of you. It happens because of your walk with Jesus - when He is living inside your heart, and you are trusting him and obeying His word. Taking the pressure completely off you and putting it on the cross gives you the confidence to walk not by your own power, but by the power of Jesus Christ. As long as you are solely dependent on yourself to save yourself, you will be a slave to your heart and all the grime, junk, wounds, and brokenness it possesses. It's when you have life in him, healing and freedom and wholeness are made possible. You are as strong as the life source to which you are connected. My friend, it gets no stronger than Jesus Christ , who is ultimate.

God did not plan to fill His world with men that blow every time the wind blows. Jesus said, "I came that they may have life and have it abundantly." John 10:10. God intended for you as a man, to thrive and grow.

In closing, yes; this will be difficult. When you as a man think or hear the word "heart" you think emotions, you think soft, you think femininity. In order for you to lead, motivate, engage, you must seek your heart and its connection with Jesus Christ.

There were once two men, and each needed to build a house. The first man was foolish, and chose to build on sandy soil where it was easy to access and easy to dig the foundations. In a few short weeks he was almost finished. The second man was wise, and chose to build his house on a rocky hill, where it was very hard to access and to dig the foundation. He spent many months building his house.

As time passed a huge storm broke upon the houses of these men. After much rain, a flood swept through the valley and the man's house that was built on the sand was swept away. But the second man who had built on the rocky hill was safe. No matter how hard it rained or how fierce the floods were his house remained solid and immovable.

Let's ask ourselves the question. What's the foundation of our life? Are we like the foolish man, are our lives built on sand? The story above is from the Matthew 7:24-27 where the Bible says: "Everyone then who hears these words of mine and does them will be like a wise man who built his house on the rock. And the rain fell, and the floods came, and the winds blew and beat on that house, but it did not fall, because it had been founded on the rock. And everyone who hears these words of mine and does not do them will be like a foolish man who built his house on the sand. And the rain fell, and the floods came, and the winds blew and beat against that house, and it fell, and great was the fall of it."

Jesus said that whoever heard his words and obeyed Him, would be like a wise man who built on a rock. And that house could never be torn down!!! It could never be moved! If we only hear the wonderful words of Jesus and yet still go our own way, we are like a foolish person, who builds his house on the sand! Just think about that. Who would want to build a house on a sand-dune? It sounds very foolish doesn't it? Perhaps the foolish man thought he was safe? His house was standing to start with and it was cozy and warm inside, everything was going just fine. But when the floods came he had no hope! His house fell flat, and great was the fall of it.

What about our lives? When Satan brings temptations and trials to us, it may feel like we are being battered by a flood. The Bible refers to the enemy coming in like a flood: Isaiah 59:19**...when the enemy shall come in like a flood...**

Perhaps you've found yourself standing on sand before. When the flood of temptation or trial comes, you fall flat like that foolish man. Don't be discouraged! Let's choose to be like the wise man who listens to what Jesus tells us in the Bible and does what He says! And when we listen and obey Jesus, what rock are we building our lives on? The LORD is my rock and my fortress and my deliverer, my God, my rock, in whom I take refuge, my shield, and the horn of my salvation, my stronghold. (Psalm 18:2).1. Corinthians 3:11 **For no one can lay a foundation other than that which is laid, which is Jesus Christ.**

Jesus is our Rock! He is the firm foundation that we can build our lives upon. And if we obey Jesus, and everything He tells us in his word, the Bible, we have the assurance that no matter what flood beats upon us, no matter how fierce the storms of this life may get we will never fall, we will never be moved.

God wants us to build securely upon the eternal Rock, the word of God. We have been only hearers long enough. Let us now put the important lessons of Christ into practice. He who is a hearer and not a doer of the word, Christ compares to the man who built his house upon the sand. It needs only the storm of temptation to break upon such, and the foundation they supposed so secure is swept away. How great is the loss to these souls! They might have had eternal life--a life that measures with the life of God--had they built upon the firm foundation. Be THIS MAN.

Community / Brotherhood

During this crazy journey called life you meet friends and lose friends for a variety of reasons. You choose who you build your network around and ultimately your family. I am sure you heard the saying before that you are who you hang out with, or you are the average of the 5 people you spend the most time with. So my question to you is who are your top 5 friends? Who do you look up too? I have been lucky enough to have a few good friends that push me to become a better person. They influence me daily to change for the better. I have also been blessed to be the person that some people have looked up too and influence their lives for the better. As you go through life we all have choices. Choices that end up creating our own identity and human being. Part of some of the choices that we are faced with every day is discovered by the friends you call your brothers. Some friends will be anchors that try and drag you down to the bottom of the ocean as you try to swim as hard as you can to just stay afloat. Others will be lifting you up to push you to become a better you. As we mentioned in this book a better you, is a person that you are happy at looking at the mirror too. The person you envision yourself to become.

To accomplish this goal it is important that you build your brotherhood around these philosophies. We as human beings are meant to build communities and socialize with other human beings.

Every day you come into contact with a lot of different people. Have you ever met someone that did something to make your day and affect it in a positive way? Now on the other hand, have you ever met someone that just made it worse? Your actions affect everything and everyone around you. Whether you are being nice to someone on the subway, holding the door for a random person, dating someone, or just being someone's friend. Every time you come in contact with someone you are being a factor in their life, whether it is a positive one or a negative one. Talk about a responsibility; you literally hold the power to change the world, to build your community for the better.

You control your actions by your mood and by being in touch with your spirit and the heart that beats inside of you. You have a lion heart beating inside your body waiting to explode on the world and make a difference. Every day, every time you talk and come in contact with another living creature. How cool is that!! The power of belief in oneself is a critical building block to achieving happiness.

When you open your eyes to the world and believe in yourself the possibilities are endless. You are capable of achieving your wildest dreams. You have the skills to achieve them. There is a power inside all of us that if we unlock it, if you have the courage to unlock it, we can achieve the impossible. The only catch is you have to believe it. You have to live it. You have to be committed. The key is to attach emotion to your life. Be happy, be excited. If I tell you live today like it is the best day of your life will you? If there is not a burning belief deep down inside your body you will not believe it. There will never be another person like you in the world who has your mind, your body, and your spirit all rolled into one. Who you were yesterday does not decide where you will be tomorrow. The person you are today decides that. So find out what you want in this life and go get it. I want you to spend 15 minutes just sitting by yourself in silence and think about what would make you happy. Picture it, envision it, believe in it, and now go get it. If you do not know how it is okay, you will find a way. The littlest changes can make the biggest impact on your life.

Everything in your body is connected. You hear a lot of athletes and sport commentators talk about the mental aspect of the "game." What you think about yourself and the world around you is your reality. If you think you cannot achieve more, make a difference in this world, or bring value to your love ones…well then that's the truth. Everything you think gets ingrained into your body and becomes your reality. I read a quote by Dwayne "The Rock" Johnson the other day that stuck with me. "Just be better today than you were yesterday." Think about that for a second. How powerful is that, any improvement is an improvement? If the farthest you have ever ran with our stopping was a mile and today you did just one more step then that is awesome. When you wake up every day you have a fresh start to be committed to yourself and your love ones, to be the best "you" that you can be. The best thing about this is the fact that yesterday did not matter and neither does tomorrow, just today. I have trained a lot of people in my life on the basics of working out and most of the time it always starts out the same. I will do it on Monday. The problem with waiting until Monday is that Monday never comes. Just like the sign, "free beer tomorrow," well when you go back to get free beer, the signs still says "free beer tomorrow." We want you to make a commitment to yourself right now. A commitment to the words of Dwayne Johnson, a commitment to take the next step, even if it's a small one. Whenever you are putting in effort to better your life you attract good fortune to yourself. My old outside salesmen Austin always said to me, good things happen to good people and good things navigate towards you when you are putting in the effort. We believe in you, we have faith in you, we are here to support you and help you piece together the pieces that are missing in your life. One step at a time, one mile at a time, until you have crossed oceans. We have created a company devoted to helping you have access to the resources to grow and inspire others around you. Reading this book is a great step in the right direction but it is only a step, if you take a step in the right direction and then stop, you are almost where you started from. The key is to keep going, to keep growing, to be devoted to yourself, to love yourself, and to believe in yourself.

NOTES

1. Lewis, Robert. A Man and His Dream. Vol. 1. Little Rock: Authentic Manhood, 2012.
2. Lewis, Robert. A Man and His Dream. Vol. 1. Little Rock: Authentic Manhood, 2012.
3. Lewis, Robert. A Man and His Dream. Vol. 1. Little Rock: Authentic Manhood, 2012.
4. Lewis, Robert. A Man and His Dream. Vol. 1. Little Rock: Authentic Manhood, 2012.
5. Lewis, Robert. A Man and His Dream. Vol. 1. Little Rock: Authentic Manhood, 2012.
6. Lewis, Robert. A Man and His Dream. Vol. 1. Little Rock: Authentic Manhood, 2012.
7. Lewis, Robert. A Man and His Dream. Vol. 1. Little Rock: Authentic Manhood, 2012.
8. Lewis, Robert. A Man and His Dream. Vol. 1. Little Rock: Authentic Manhood, 2012.
9. Lewis, Robert. A Man and His Dream. Vol. 1. Little Rock: Authentic Manhood, 2012.

ABOUT THE AUTHORS

Akai J. Jackson

Akai Jackson earned a Bachelor's Degree in Entertainment Business and an Associate's in Recording Arts from Full Sail University, in Winter Park, Florida. He is internationally certified through Premier Global, and holds many of the top rated certifications nationally recognized in the United States. He has made his mark in the fitness industry for over ten years. He has succeeded as a personal trainer and an athletic conditioning coach. From 2006-2012, he was a personal training manager for the fastest growing privately owned and operated health club - Lifestyle Family Fitness. He had an affluent athletic career playing high profile basketball at the high school level as well as at the college level. Akai currently serves as the Strength and Conditioning Coach for the University of Central Florida, Men's Lacrosse Team.

Since he has been a part of the fitness industry he has earned numerous sales awards, as well as selling and generating over 3 million dollars in personal training. He was a vital role in the standard of excellence set forth by Premier Health and Fitness out of Annapolis, Maryland. He has a devout passion for changing lives and making a positive influence in the community. Akai Jackson is one of the most sought after fitness professionals in the industry. He has personally helped many high school, college, and professional athletes. He is a devout Christian who facilitates groups within men's ministry. He has a heart for the development of men and their mission for life.

Allan E. Sobie

When you think of Allan the word natural born leader comes to mind. With over 10 years of sales and management experience with top fortune 2,000 companies including Ferguson Enterprises, Océ North America, Canon, and First Data, it is no wonder why he continues to reach new heights. He has the dedication to his professional career as well as willingness to grow which has lead him to obtain many top awards such as President's Club and is continually on top of the sales rankings. His selling success dates as far back at the age of 7, where he was honored 4 years in a row as one of the top salesmen in the Boy Scouts of America. I have never met a person with a bigger heart and passion all rolled up in one human being who cares more about others then he does himself. Where if you looked up the definition of Lionheart in the dictionary, I wouldn't be surprised if there was a picture of him. The type of leader who will jump out of his car in 100 degree weather, in a suit, on his way to a business meeting, to help push a car off the road to help the driver. I know this because I have seen it firsthand. It is this drive and passion for helping others that lead him to become the Co-Founder of Perfection Development Group, a company devoted to helping change the lives of all of its clients. Allan graduated from University of Central Florida with dual bachelor degrees in Business Administration and Marketing, and has a diploma in Sports Nutrition from the Shaw Academy. Allan has trained and competed in many sports and ultra-endurance events and has personally trained, coached, and mentored many people throughout his life time. Allan resides in Colorado with his beautiful and amazing wife Kelli, dog Noodle, and cats Bubba and Rasha.

www.ingramcontent.com/pod-product-compliance
Lightning Source LLC
LaVergne TN
LVHW021355080426
835508LV00020B/2286